GW01043883

And Now It's Sables

ALSO BY GINETTE SPANIER

It Isn't All Mink

Ginette Spanier

And Now It's Sables

PREFACE BY
Maurice Chevalier

ILLUSTRATED

Robert Hale & Company

© *Ginette Spanier 1970*

First published in Great Britain March 1970

Reprinted March 1970

SBN 7091 1240 8

Robert Hale & Company
63 Old Brompton Road
London S.W.7

PRINTED IN GREAT BRITAIN BY
LOWE AND BRYDONE (PRINTERS) LTD LONDON

Contents

Illustrations

Preface

Mister Robert Hale, the publisher of *And Now It's Sables*
written by my friend Ginette Spanier, insists, so she tells
me, that I should write the preface of her book; and in
English with all that. I take it as a wonderful compliment
because, after all, Ginette knows, I presume, all the best
writers in the world. I will go as far as saying that she
knows all the best people in every line from anywhere and
even probably, soon, in the moon, when they come out
of hiding. No doubt she could easily choose a better
writing name.

So, I accept willingly because of what Mister Robert
Hale thinks of me and because Ginette and her husband are
to my mind two 'séducteurs' of the best of artistic 'séducteurs' to be found in the Celebrity Book. For that is their
most indisputable performance which is astonishing to
the point of uniqueness; win affectionately people who
are almost sick of being too much sought after and so
successful that they run the risk of becoming bored with
the whole business.

How does she do it? That's in her, probably.

I don't know anybody to compare with her in that
respect. She is a really attractive woman of her age.
Friendly, warm, strong and gracious. Between her Balmain responsibilities, her travels and conferences in every
part of the world, taking care of the friends she makes, and

keeps, wherever she goes, and last but not least, the affectionate harmony that she creates in her home life between her and Paul-Emile, her doctor husband. She works harder than most great women I know of.

I am, myself, a loner, seldom go to parties. Feel kind of embarrassed, also on the stage. My best professional job has been doing one-man shows with the only assistance of a pianist, and all over this planet. And now at eighty-one it's getting rather worse. But, just a minute . . . not a cold loner . . . no . . . a warm loner when I come across the authentic.

And I can testify that each time Ginette phoned to ask me to come for a drink at her apartment, I have met great people totally at ease, relaxed and utterly lovable, as if we needed these intimate meetings to all feel brothers, sisters and real children of the stage.

I think it started one day with Danny Kaye whom I had met already in New York. Seeing him at Ginette's home, made me know him so much more. Since then we have become real pals. Another time it was Laurence Olivier and Vivien Leigh, and we talked and talked with those two greats as if I was a born cockney. Another wonderful feeling. As you can see, that was already long ago.

Nobody is more different from me than Noël Coward and still there's something very warm and real about our esteem for each other always through Ginette. And Alfred Lunt and Lynn Fontane, American royalty of the stage, talking quietly, deeply and beautifully about our craft. It was a treat, thanks to that particular Ginette and Paul-Emile atmosphere. With them around I can come out of my shell and force my timidity to open up. What a grand feeling.

It was also thanks to Ginette that I could again renew some beautiful moments with Claudette Colbert after having worked with her in the thirties in two films: *The Big Pond* and *The Smiling Lieutenant*. As attractive as Claudette was at the time, and believe me, she was, I don't know if she is not more impressive today, looking so physically and normally splendid.

I hope these meetings will go on for years and years and that Ginette will also help me to meet some of the new English and American stars that I already admire before I can feel sure that I love them.

Go on being your splendid self, Dear Ginette. Go on showing our English and American friends, a French woman who is the epitome of attractiveness, class, talent, gentleness, courage and guts.

Show us all how one can grow in years and grow in quality, week by week, day by day. Bless you both Ginette and Paul-Emile and keep on the good work. You are an example of the constant *émerveillement* of being lucky enough to be alive.

Paris

Maurice Chevalier

To

NOËL COWARD

"Thank you for half a century of joys"

I

The Lace Curtain

When I was a child I lived on the fourth floor of a quiet block of flats, in a quiet bourgeois street, in a quiet bourgeois quarter of Paris. The only unquiet element of that quiet street was the Board School opposite. I would look down from the window and see the children pour out into the street in a noisy, friendly crowd, all of them wearing black overalls. In those days in France 'poor children' wore black overalls at school, even the boys. I saw them shout and play and kick their thick brown boots against the pavement, whilst there I was, up behind my lace curtain, in the safe, peaceful warmth of our comfortable home, wearing a dress with a ribbon run through the waist, real lace on my petticoat and spotless white shoes on my feet. I, who wasn't allowed out of the flat by myself, even onto the landing, far less into the street.

Those kids in black overalls shouting in the street—
they represented freedom to me. One day, I'd be one of
them.

Two people in my whole life understood this passionate
longing of mine and helped me to get from behind my
lace curtain.

The first was what, for lack of a better word, we'll call
my governess: Muriel Chapman, Irish, gay, brilliant, our
wonderful Deedee. She arrived in our house on my sixth
birthday, and is still a beloved member of our family.

The second, after an interval of about forty years, was
Nancy Spain.

The first helped me over my childhood. The second
over middle-age.

In the intervening years, two wars came and went.
During the first one, in 1916, the Spaniers, mother, father
and three little daughters, moved to England.

In the thirties I started earning my living—as a shopgirl at Fortnum and Mason's in Piccadilly. I climbed the
échelons of my trade until, after many vicissitudes, I
reached my present position—*directrice* of the famous Paris
fashion house of Pierre Balmain.

Just before the Second World War I married a Frenchman and moved back to France. Three months after my
marriage I was cut off from everything I loved most:
England, my family, my friends. The Germans had
invaded France. During four and a half years my husband
and I were hunted like animals, but most of this I have
described in my first book *It Isn't All Mink*.

With the exception of the German occupation of
France, I have always had a wonderful time, making
friends everywhere. Many of these belong to the theatre.
The theatre, since the moment when for the first time I
saw a curtain rise on a stage (it was at the Scala Theatre in
London for *The Purple Mask* with Matheson Lang), has
been my great love. There does lurk inside me some
resentment at my not being on the other side of the foot-

lights, but the resentment is entirely aimed at myself for not having 'had a go'. There is a gutlessness there which I despise in myself. It's the Pisces in me—those two little fish pulling in opposite directions. I'm a true Pisces—7th March—and, believe me, that's no sign to load a baby with at birth. You go ahead triumphantly, and then that cowardly, beastly, sly, rotten little second fish tugging the other way impedes your progress, when he doesn't trip you up altogether. I despise that second little fish. And when he gets the better of me I despise Ginette Spanier.

So, until 1956, I had a good life in spite of a little nagging dissatisfaction hidden away which might possibly have grown into bitterness as I grew older. Until Nancy Spain appeared. She gave me the courage to go down into that street, not very spectacularly I have to admit, but down there just the same. She made me write my autobiography, and this radically changed my existence. Mind you, it did not surprise me that a whole new phase of my life should unfold at a time when I ought normally to be settling back into middle-age. I have always believed in my star. I still do, most fervently. I am certain that the future holds many fascinating experiences for me in spite of the advancing years.

This book is not a sequel to *It Isn't All Mink*. It is the book of a different woman, one who finally achieved her black overall, her thick brown boots and incidentally her sable coat.

2

The Village

Nancy Spain used to compare my mind to a pool in which little gleaming fish—my thoughts—darted about just below the surface without apparent order or reason. There are some people like Noël Coward whose minds are so rapier-fast that when one is with them shorthand thinking and talking is a great temptation, but in the ordinary way I do try and discipline myself to finish a sentence before going on to the next. When I am alone, however, the little fish dart about uncontrolled. Therefore this book may at times be a little disconnected. This is a warning.

Although I always notice every detail about people, 'things' have a way of passing me by. One of my friends used to shout at me, "Look and Register". The other day I realized I had no idea where one of our most valuable pieces of furniture had got to—exquisite marqueterie.

Although I don't really care about possessions, and antiques mean nothing to me except ruined stockings on jagged edges, I thought it was silly to have lost it. I looked all over the flat before I realized that it was sitting there between two of the windows in the drawing-room—just where it had been for months! Every single day we have our meals in the drawing-room because the real dining-room has been turned into the consulting-room. In France, doctors practise in their homes. My husband is a French doctor. Paul-Emile Seidmann. He's tall and calm, intelligent and wears glasses. Attractive. The house, one of those big old-fashioned French apartment houses, is on a corner. Our flat goes all the way round. Many of the rooms are circular. We get the sun from early morning until, in the evening, it pops round the Arc de Triomphe before setting.

The Arc de Triomphe is just up on the right at the corner of my avenue. I should, of course, give it a glance as I dash off to work every morning, but I am in too much of a hurry.

It is downhill on my way to work and a terrible grind uphill as I walk home exhausted at the end of the day. A pity it's not the other way round. Most days I do this trip four times. In France everybody goes home to lunch, a nice friendly habit, and this walk gives me the only fresh air and exercise I get for weeks on end.

I rush out of the house in the morning down a first short street. I cannot tell you anything about that street because I'm too busy trying to wake up, pulling on my gloves, opening my umbrella when it's raining. In the short street I have to shake off my early morning irritations: the maid who asks questions at the wrong moment (it's always the wrong moment for me in the mornings), the people who call me on the telephone when I am trying to get ready:

"I'm ringing you at home because I don't want to disturb you at work."

At work one is organized to cope with disturbance, but at home! Breakfast in bed listening to the BBC from

B

London is sacred. Those last precious, fleeting moments of peace and privacy slipping away like sand in an egg-timer. I loathe getting up in the morning. When I did "Desert Island Discs", in answer to the question: "What in civilization would you be most pleased to leave behind?", without hesitation I answered, "Getting up in the morning." Those-who-like-the-morning, what makes them so pleased with themselves? It isn't a virtue. What's so great or so clever about it? "Aren't you up yet, lazy?" they say over the telephone. "Shut up", I want to moan, "and allow us-who-loathe-the-morning to stew quietly in our private horror and climb out of it slowly, painfully and in silence."

The rue Magellan, the next street, is a typically French street, anonymous and darkish, with anonymous, darkish apartment buildings on either side. This is my street of Decisions. By the time I reach it, I'm awake. In the rue Magellan I have taken decisions which have altered the whole of my life. "Shall I? If I don't, I'm a fool. All right, don't, but don't grumble afterwards." It is always the things I haven't done in life which I regret.

The rue Magellan is very different in the winter and in the summer. During the long winter months it is closed and almost shuttered to the outside world but, as spring appears, the windows open tentatively one by one, and finally the rue Magellan wakes up. *Concierges* and dreadful plants appear in the ground-floor windows. Sometimes canaries. At number twelve the arrogant, despising Siamese cat stretches his limbs and takes up his summer quarters on the window sill. Pop music emerges from the open windows of the studios of Radio Monte Carlo.

Winter and summer I walk down the rue Magellan talking to myself and taking decisions.

Then crash—bang—LIFE . . . the avenue Georges V! Traffic in every direction. Rich cars; small cars; bicycles, delivery vans—and me trying to slip my way in between them. Dangerous. I go everywhere by aeroplane in every kind of weather, and people exclaim at how courageous I am. When I say that it is in the hysteria of the Paris traffic that I am frightened, they smile and say how witty I am. What's the use of trying to explain?

In the avenue Georges V, there in front of me, is the first chestnut tree to sprout tiny buds. His brothers still look dead and grey, and just that one tree comes to life at the very moment when one feels winter will never end. That's the time I risk getting run over the most, because, as I cross the street, my eyes are fixed on the branches which, suddenly, are not bare any more. That tree is also the first to go brown and burnt at the very beginning of August when all the others are still green. Its leaves hang down like dried seaweed. I love autumn.

And then starts *my* village—the rue François Ier, the street where I work, this street which is now the main artery of the Haute Couture since it moved away from the rue de la Paix near the Opera, which was in the old Gigi days of the Couture. From all over the world people dress up to come to our village, even if it's only to look longingly at the windows or to study the famous names over the doors. Not us, whose working home it is. We are inclined to be a bit sloppy sartorially as we rush down the street, our arms full of parcels, hatless, waving to our street companions right and left. When we're not in a hurry, it is one long gossip.

There on the left is Delaporte, the cleaners. I rush in, dump a dress on the counter, and a pair of ex-white kid gloves and say, "*Bonjour tout le monde*", and I'm off. If you want to see the latest fashions, all you have to do is step into Madame Delaporte's shop. The great couture houses send her their dresses to be cleaned. There they hang next to each other: Balmain, Balenciaga, Dior, Saint Laurent, Venet, those exquisite dresses, deadly rivals, created in the utmost secrecy, Capulet and Montagu children, suddenly hanging cheek by jowl in a tidy row.

Monsieur Delaporte has one terrible fault: he's lazy. He will not send us 'habitués' our accounts.

I shout as I go out of the door, "Tell Monsieur to make out my bill!"

But months pass, and I float along in a fool's paradise until one day—a bill for £100! Objects sent out dirty and returned clean, all listed in a spiky French handwriting on blue paper. Monsieur Delaporte has woken up. No joke. I wish I hadn't reminded him.

There are times when I have debts all down the street: rent-paying day, tax-due week or just the usual old end of the month. The French are not the Olympic champions of credit-giving, but it's different in our village.

I shout, *"Je n'ai pas le sou."*

And they shrug their shoulders and say, *"Eh bien, ça attendra. Vous en faites pas!"* They have, it must be admitted, seen me pass up and down the street these last twenty years.

I love spending money, so whenever I have any I spend it . . . so I never have any. My father was like me—we were alike in many ways. The rest of the family keep thinking about their old age. They have always tried to hammer this principle into me, but it doesn't work. The present has always been so important to me. And somehow I've had the feeling I would be able to earn money even when quite old. I still feel that way with old age creeping up on me. I love the sport of earning money. The excitement. Not to speak of the exquisite results thereof. Earning money is the only sport in which I indulge.

All this time I'm jogging down the rue François Ier. In this street, the furrier is one of my favourites. Good-looking, well-dressed, rather dashing, he has never, in spite of selling sables and minks in one of the most elegant parts of Paris, given up the age-old habit of the Jewish merchant which is to do most of his business out in the street. Hatless, overcoatless in every kind of weather (he has very expensive cashmere sweaters) there he is, gossiping on the pavement in front of his luxurious shop, or drinking endless cups of coffee at the café on the corner. After ten years of seeing each other almost daily we smiled, after twelve we talked, after fourteen he kissed my hand, now he kisses my hand and my cheek. With many gestures he tells everyone, "This is my friend." Regularly he asks me why I don't borrow one of his beautiful fur coats when I go out in the evening. "You'd be such great publicity!" Smilingly I remind him that I work at No. 44 rue François Ier, not No. 56, and if there's any publicity going around it will be for Balmain. "Leave Balmain", he says, "come and work for me. You're the girl I need to run my business." I smile and say, "Maybe," and dash off down the road.

Without any doubt, for me the most important shop on my way to work is Georgel, the hairdresser. I suppose I have run in there on an average three times a week for almost twenty years, and three times a week for all those years I have been greeted with smiles and a Big Hello, and customers have been dropped so that I can be looked after. I only got around to Georgel's some time after my arrival in the village. At the beginning I was still an outsider, intimidated, and so hard at work learning my job in the couture that I did not think of spending time on anything else, certainly not on etceteras like having my hair done every few days.

In Paris we carry on terribly about our hair. We spend a great deal of time and money on having it dyed, washed, set and combed out. Even my husband, who would hardly notice if I wore a long dress in the daytime (I exaggerate), is apt to say, "*Tu es mal coiffée.* Shall I drop you at Georgel's in the car on your way to work?"

If I feel I am *mal coiffée* my confidence evaporates like steam. Woman's confidence is gossamer stuff, the least thing shatters it: chipped varnish on a nail, a ladder in one's stocking, an inch of hem undone, imperfect hair most of all. There must be something deeply psychological about hair. All that hysteria about Samson and the Beatles.

When I was a teenager, girls, at a certain stage of their evolution, 'put their hair up'. My turn came. Delighted at this proof of my adulthood, I proudly wore my hair in a bun in the nape of my neck, with, in front, my parting in the middle. Very classical. Before that, my raven locks had been held back in a slide and, one riotous year, tied with a largish black taffeta bow. In front there was always that parting in the middle.

Every autumn I went to Paris and stayed with my relations. I used to buy all my clothes in Paris. I was a very dressy girl. My shopping did not lead my footsteps towards an establishment of Haute Couture, but to one of those little dressmakers for which Paris is famous, who shamelessly copy the star dresses of the season at an interesting price, the breed of '*copiste*' I now mercilessly try to root out and destroy. Had I, at that time, been told that I should one day be dressed exclusively by one of the most famous couturiers in the world, I would have fainted dead away with joy, excitement and complete disbelief.

One year, when I was in Paris, Madame Chanel decreed that we should adopt the Boyish Look—corsets thrown over the windmill and hair cut short in a style named— hush—the Shingle. In fact—Revolution! I dashed to the hairdresser's and, my eyes tight closed at the crucial moment, my heart pounding, off came my chignon. My family made a terrible fuss.

Some time later, when it was 'the thing', I grew my hair again. I wore it long all through the war because we were too poor for me to go regularly to the hairdresser and also, as we spent most of our time hiding from the Germans in small villages, there was no question of having one's hair properly cut. In those days I wore my hair in a snood because hairpins disappeared (like in *Gone With The Wind*; clever of Margaret Mitchell to have guessed that detail!). The Germans requisitioned every scrap of metal for their war effort. For instance, it was impossible to buy a new tube of toothpaste unless we brought the old empty squashed one in exchange.

When I was young, my hair was very black—dark black—and people went on about my profile. I don't like profiles. Half a face. You can't see the eyes. And then someone said I looked like Ivor Novello. This was the proudest achievement of my whole youth, and I became very pleased with my profile. Gallery girls (that's what 'fans' were called in those days) came up to me outside theatres and asked if I was Ivor Novello's sister. Ivor Novello was The Beatles of my youth. I had long daydreams about a play where Ivor Novello had to have a twin sister and suddenly a manager saw me in the street and London was at my feet. In my dreams we went everywhere together, Ivor Novello and I, to exciting places one read about in *The Tatler*, both of us with our shiny black hair and our so-alike profiles. But I never met my twin.

Although, strangely enough, the fact that I looked like him made a great difference to my life; I never really had much fun at dances. I wasn't a flirt. (How old-fashioned that word sounds now!) I think it was because my ambitions had nothing to do with the ordinary boys I met at dances. I wanted more *panache*. Then one day I went to a dull dance in Fitzjohn's Avenue, Hampstead. And there was a good-looking, elegant young man. Very different from the run of young men at my dances. Lovely cufflinks and studs, looking bored in his perfect tails. Young men wore tails a great deal in my day, but very few knew how. Tails are the most difficult things for men to carry off with chic.

The bored one came up to me and said, "Do you know that you are the exact image of Ivor Novello? Will you have the supper dance with me?"

The supper dance was a knotty problem at balls. It lasted too long. But that supper dance didn't seem too long. In fact, from that moment on I had fun. I became the toast of a whole lot of young men who didn't seem to mind a bit about my not flirting. We laughed. They were funny and brilliant and good-looking and they took me to lovely places like backstage and the 50–50 Nightclub. And I suddenly found that I could be funny, too, and my mother's friends shook their heads and said I would never get married.

I always had chic. I carried off my clothes in a very Parisian way—exotic for Hampstead. Young men would say to me in the 1925 version of 'You look smashing', "You look spiffing!" but, through it all, I realized they would often have preferred me to be a horse. Oh dear, the English with their love of animals.

But when I went around with all those attractive, beautiful, brilliant young men, I realized that not for a second did they wish I was a horse, which was nice for me. They loved my wearing black velvet when my girl friends wore shot taffeta. However, sometimes at a party I'd be standing there surrounded, when a cute little page boy passed by in a tight little uniform and I suddenly felt all alone in the middle of all those young men. Well, you can't have everything, and I had laughter in great quantity and I loved that.

To grow up a girl in England isn't easy. They don't help you with the confidence bit. But let's get back to Ivor Novello. Oddly enough, over the years, people still continued to remark that I looked exactly like him, although my hair got to be a little less black.

Half a dozen people promised to arrange a meeting, but something always happened to prevent it. Then one day I had a letter from Fabia Drake, the actress, asking Paul-Emile and me to luncheon in London. A definite date and no nonsense—and Ivor Novello was to be there. We travelled from Paris for the fateful, long-postponed meeting, only to learn that Ivor Novello had died in the night.

To go back to my hair, when I came back to a normal life after the liberation of France from the German occupation I continued to wear it in a bun at the back. It never occurred to me to change my style. For four and a half years our only thought had been to keep alive and it took time to adapt to peace. During the war, Paul-Emile and I, as Jews, had been forbidden to work, very nearly to live. After four and a half years of living in the provinces, in the country, I had to learn to live in Paris; I had to look for a job, ready to start way down again at the bottom of the ladder. I was totally unknown in France, I who had made a success in England. By a miracle I got the job at Balmain's.* There, I suddenly found myself in the middle of everything that was most elegant, most expensive, most international. I had to relearn the language of luxury. And I still kept my bun at the back of my head. Until one night I was at the Café de Paris in London dancing with Danny Kaye; I was wearing a white embroidered Balmain dress, but my hair was parted in the middle and there was that bun at the back of my head.

Danny Kaye said to me, "You look like a governess; you must cut off your bun."

I had never thought about it. It's terrible having no imagination.

Back in Paris, I went straight to Georgel's and said, "*Plus de chignon.*"

They all made a great song and dance about it. Stood around exclaiming "*On coupe les cheveux à Madame Spanier!*"

I love a song and dance.

Early on I got a grey streak in my hair. I was proud of my streak up on the right mixed in with my black hair. Then the grey invaded everywhere and the black lost its foothold in sad defeat. One day Marlene Dietrich was staying with us, and René came to do her hair in our bathroom. Marlene suddenly looked at me there in the bathroom and said in her dark gold voice:

"Who do you think you're helping with all that gwey hair?" (Marlene often can't say her Rs). René agreed. I had

_____
* See *It Isn't All Mink.*

never thought about having my hair dyed. Marlene's advice is very precious to me, especially as she's not one for interfering except on very special occasions.

So I went straight to Georgel's and said, "*Plus de cheveux gris*," and made an appointment to have my hair dyed.

I was very excited at the idea of seeing something quite new in the glass after all those years. When I got there for the operation, the appointment had been cancelled. Monsieur Georgel's orders.

He said I had too much *classe*, and that I was too *distinguée* to have my hair dyed like everybody. I was furious, after having taken the psychological plunge, to be thwarted in this way, especially as I have never been a great one for the *classe* and *distinguée* act. I just like chic. I had to wait until Monsieur Georgel went away fishing before I had my hair dyed. It's been through many shades since that day. At the moment it is 'Loving Care' No. 77. Claudette Colbert chose that colour when I was staying with her in Palm Springs in the Californian Desert.

When I arrived she said casually, "We're dining with Frank Sinatra tonight."

I'd never met Frank Sinatra.

I screamed "I must have my hair done!"

Claudette said, "I'll do it." Claudette and I are such great friends, we always have so much to talk about—half in French and half in English—that it would have been silly to waste a whole afternoon at the beauty shop.

So, we drove to the nearest drugstore and chose 'Loving Care' No. 77. Back to the bathroom basin, and Claudette dyed it, set it and even cut it.

Dyeing one's hair is a big problem. It is dangerous for an ageing lady to dye her hair too dark. She can easily look as if she's got a tight little cap on made of black boot polish.

"*Pour un oui, pour un non*," as they say in French, I run into Georgel's. In the morning on my way to work if I look a mess; in the evening on my way home if I'm going out. Eliane, who looks after me, gives me '*un coup de peigne'* (a comb-out)—five minutes, and I'm transformed. She's a wizard with a *peigne*, Eliane. She also has a sense of humour. Once a week I have 'the works'. And always everyone smiles and is sweet to me, and other customers are dropped so that I don't wait even five minutes. I'd murder Madame Spanier if I were another customer at Georgel's!

Across the road from Georgel's is the *marchand de couleurs*—the French for hardware shop. I am very attached to the hardware shop. The son of the owner is attractive, and also amiable, even if I only go in there to buy a refill battery for my radio. To be amiable in a shop—and that includes the shop where I work—is absolutely indispensable. I was trained that way at Fortnum and Mason's in 1930, and I try to carry on the tradition now that I am in a bossy position. People say that the atmosphere at Balmain's is quite exceptional. I have stopped going to some shops in my village because of people being disagreeable to me. If I'm going to give my good, hard-earned money to someone, they'd better be civil and pleasant. I do not belong to the grumble-grumble-and-do-nothing-about-it school of thought. This attitude is very French. They even have a word for it—*râler*. Everybody *râles* and does nothing about it. I don't *râle*. Sometimes I shout, and I stop giving them my money.

Speaking of the hardware shop, I do not feel as passionately as Marlene Dietrich does when it comes to hardware stores. In her *ABC* she writes, "I'd rather go to a hardware store than to the opera. And I like opera. The hardware store's only rival is the stationery store."

Now you're talking, my lovely Marlene. Luckily for me, and my fortune, the stationery shop is a block down one of the side streets, so I don't pass it every day on my way to work. I have to make a special trip to go there.

Once I am inside the stationery store I'm a dead duck.

Again in her *ABC*, Marlene writes:

People who adore stationery stores are like dope addicts about paper clips, paper clamps, ring clips, bulldog clips, Magic Markers, china markers, felt-tip pens, Scotch tapes, Mystic tapes, varieties of pads, notebooks with spirals on top, notebooks with spirals on the side, short, wide, long, narrow. Paper devoted to erasers, paper-thick, stiff, hard, soft, rough, large like canvas, surfaces like linen or pigskin. The addict buys feverishly all he needs and all he does not need and has absolutely no use for. He just cannot leave it in the store.

Two things I take exception to. Marlene has left out those thick transparent folders of every colour for filing one's papers, and I won't have Scotch tape pushed in among the common herd. Scotch tape is the aristocrat of the stationery store. If one day I have to choose between Scotch Whisky and Scotch Tape, it will be a soul-crushing decision.

The boys in the spectacle shop are sweet. They're great at giving credit, just as I'm great at losing my glasses and at breaking them.

I do not even mention the *patisserie*, its windows gleaming with cakes of every kind. It means nothing to me. I've never had a sweet tooth. To my husband the *dolce* part of the meal is what he enjoys best. After almost thirty years of living together he still cannot believe it when, at the end of the meal, I shake my head as the sweets are presented to me and go straight on to coffee from the meat course. Unless, of course, there is cheese. I am very lucky that only a few minutes from where I work is one of the great cheese shops of Paris. A shop in which there are 133 varieties of cheese displayed on clean, scrubbed marble shelves: cheeses of every shape and every size, cheeses from every corner of France, cheeses made from cow's milk, from goat's milk, cheeses ready to be eaten today, cheeses which must be kept for tomorrow. The food that I provide for my husband and my guests may sometimes be lacking in subtlety and Cordon Bleu perfection, but my cheeses are always beyond reproach.

Some shops on my route indulge in the dreadful habit common in France, of closing at lunch time. Rattling at a locked door at lunch time when I have only a very limited shopping time rouses me to passionate hatred. It's so undemocratic. The other day I went to the big church down the street to say a little prayer, and there was a notice on the door, "Closed from 13.00 hours–15.00 hours". Haven't they ever heard of working in shifts?

Some of the shopkeepers when I pass down the street look terribly depressed. They wave at me in a gloomy sort of way and I feel I ought to go in and buy something just to cheer them up. So I cross over.

I run a mile from people who make me feel guilty. It's like those who consider you have a 'duty' towards them. Is there in the whole of the English language, a drier, colder more soulless word than duty? "I must go and visit so-and-so, it's my duty." *Quelle horreur!* If it's a pleasure to go and see them, then it isn't a duty any more and, therefore, devoid of noble self-sacrifice. 'Self-sacrifice' makes me feel pretty sick, too. Please, when I'm old and lonely, let nobody come to see me out of 'duty'. If I'm a reasonably clean old lady, and not too much of a bore, if I have retained my interest in people, maybe now and then someone will come and visit me because they like me. But leave me alone with my television set if it's out of 'duty' that you are coming to see me.

Nor is 'to visit' my favourite expression either. It smells of good works.

The hub, the centre, the focal point of the village is the café on the corner, 'La Belle Ferronnière' (The Beautiful Ironworker), or 'La Belle Féfé' for short, called after the mistress of François I, king of France in the sixteenth century and patron of our street. Here is concentrated the life of the neighbourhood. At the first ray of sunshine the pavement is so crowded that you have to walk in the gutter to get by. There sit sipping and trying to attract attention the 'with-it' girls and boys, sunburnt at whatever time of year it is, the starlets and models, the would-be starlets, the would-be models, all dressed very much alike in the uniform of the month. Small open sports cars cruise slowly by. People wave and shout to each other. Triumphantly, from across the road stroll the *Paris-Match* boys, a breed in themselves, conscious of their power, their youth, their courage, their attraction. Roger, the *chasseur* from Georgel's, darts in and out of the traffic carrying a tray laden with glasses and sandwiches for the ladies sitting under the dryers. I wave to a friend or two, throw a letter into the letter-box and get to work.

Walking home in the evening I am so tired that I notice nothing, see nobody. I don't care what I look like, whether I've any lipstick left on, whether I look a mess, who sees me as I walk by 'La Belle Féfé'. I totter up the hill. I fall into the door of 70 Avenue Marceau. Up in the tiny lift, fiddle for my keys. I'm home, and its quiet and peaceful and spacious.

Years and years of it, and still my husband rushes at me before I've had time to take off my coat.

"What happened today at Balmain's?"

I snap. I'm rude. I'm exhausted. Zero hour.

Off with my shoes. Lie flat on the bed for ten minutes. And then quick, quick, quick, my lovely Waterford glass, four enormous lumps of ice, a strong dose of Scotch, a splash of soda, my red corduroy velvet arm-chair, my feet up on the stool in front of me, the cold, cold glass in my hand.

Re-lax-a-tion.

Come on, Paul-Emile, what's new?

3

More a Saloon than a Salon

My flat is the opposite of what I really like. I love low ceilings. My flat has high ceilings and beautiful proportions; an oblong drawing-room with four big windows looking out on a view of Paris which looks like an Utrillo; and a round hall. From some of our windows we can see the Arc de Triomphe, from some others the Eiffel Tower. My flat has many rooms, some of which we don't use, which is an awful admission for me, who hates waste. Every year we do up one room, but there is always another which has grown shabby, and somehow we never catch up. The carpet in the hall is bright red. It's the first thing you see as you come in, acres of lovely red carpet. It hasn't been there very long, the old one grew shabby and once, when Laurence Olivier came to stay with us, before we knew where we were, there was the lovely new red carpet for a Christmas present.

Outside the front door of the apartment is a mat with Dr. P-E. S. written across it in red letters to show the patients where the doctor lives. France is full of old-fashioned prejudices like it's not being chic for a successful doctor to have a plate on the door, but it's all right to have his initials on the mat!

There's plenty that's nice about the flat. You walk round the corner and you're in the Champs Elysées. Like living off Piccadilly Circus. That's a relief after having spent one's youth in Golders Green and praying nobody would see you home because you knew they'd get sick of you before they got half-way. Also there's nothing poky about the apartment. There's no question about it, you get used to space and spreading yourself around. And the walls are thick so you never hear the neighbours. I only hope the neighbours don't hear me when I listen to the English radio half the night. I suffer from insomnia.

The central heating in the building is great. It mostly is in France. I love good central heating although my English friends find it far too hot and say they're going to faint. Icy draughts make me feel vicious.

The building was constructed around 1890—the exact *époque* of the French farce. In our flat there are doors everywhere. It is easy to imagine people rushing in and out like *A Flea In Her Ear* or *Love Among the Pigeons*: ladies letting out their lovers by one door and the irate husband coming in by the other. When we moved in, the sitting-room which is not a big room had five doors. We blocked up three and made them into bookcases. The big, oval drawing-room had a painted ceiling with a blue sky and pink cherubs. We painted over the sky and the cherubs. The drawing-room is a really beautiful room with a star in the middle of the polished parquet flooring and two sets of rather majestic double doors. It is a spacious room, what Americans would call 'gracious'. When Noël Coward wrote *Nude With Violin*, he insisted on the set-designer copying our drawing-room for the act which took place in Paris. They came over from England to photograph it. It was funny watching Sir John Gielgud on the stage in our own home.

When we have people in to drinks they just will not go into the drawing-room, they prefer to squash into the sitting-room even though we open the double doors between the two rooms. I'm on their side, but Claudette Colbert disapproves. She prefers the drawing-room and, to encourage us to use it, she brought us a beautiful carpet from Portugal, lovely yellows and greys. Our friends are very carpet-conscious for us. And generous.

Of my friends, Claudette Colbert is one of the closest. She is intelligent and attractive and funny and she and I share a built-in love of life and of people. Now, alas, since the death of her husband in 1966, there is an irremediable sadness underlying Claudette's gaiety. Her husband, Jack Pressman, was a brilliant professor of laryngology. They were married for over thirty years.

Claudette has just taken a flat in Paris. It will be nice for me to have her almost next door for a goodly part of the year, instead of holiday meetings in the most varied parts of the world.

Claudette Colbert is a perfectionist, I might even say she is an addict in that direction. I am NOT, and that's no idle statement. At the beginning one tries to run around and help Claudette in whatever it is she is doing, but after some absolutely hopeless efforts, because she does things quicker and better than anyone else and has some very determined ideas into the bargain, one sits back and rises above the whole situation whilst Madam Colbert rushes about complicating her life in her own inimitable manner.

I am not proud of the fact that I am not a good 'house-wife', but I'm a real fool in the kitchen. I think it is because I don't really care about food. I could live on boiled eggs and cheese and cold chicken. I also love porridge. This is

c

a terrible confession from someone living in Paris where food is one of the important considerations of life. Fortunately for me, my French husband is a darling about this blind spot of mine. He understands and enjoys good food, good wine, but he couldn't make less fuss about the whole thing.

Even though I'm a fool in the kitchen, I'm not a fool in the house. I'm for ever tidying and organizing. I love it. And my house runs smoothly enough. This is very important with the Doctor receiving his patients in the flat and me out at work all day. I must say I have been marvellously lucky at finding 'treasures' to help me. They have looked after us beautifully and have really made all the difference to our lives.

The sitting-room is where we 'live'. When we're alone we even eat there on a card table in front of the television set. It is an intimate room with English furniture, a comfortable English sofa covered in green corduroy (its springs, I am afraid, need mending), two beautiful large English armchairs, mahogany and bright red corduroy velvet, and an English club fender with two little red seats. It's stupid that we never have a fire in the fireplace but I've never got round to organizing it. I've always wanted to. It would make the room even cosier. There are hundreds of books in bookshelves round the walls— maybe thousands, many with beautiful leather bindings. Paul-Emile's great passion is books. (He reads *War and Peace* once a year. I find that rather affected, but he's in love with Natasha. I love *War and Peace* myself, but I don't read it every year.) Paul-Emile's books are French and Russian, mine are English.

Over the fireplace is our most beautiful picture. A Loiseau. It is such a beautiful picture that I said to Paul-Emile, "I'm growing old. I now have a possession that I would be sad to lose in a fire." (Except for about two things which could fit into my pocket, I have no sense of possession.) Loiseau was a pupil of Pissaro so he's not

quite an Impressionist. Just 'post'. But it's in the right
direction compared to the rest of our pictures, all of which
I would gladly sell to buy another Loiseau. Except one—
a Dimitrienko—almost abstract, reds and blacks, dripping
red paint like blood. It's supposed to be a *Calvaire en
Bretagne*, but to me it has all the suffering of the German
occupation.

When we are just Paul-Emile and me in the sitting-
room, I sit in one of the big red velvet armchairs with my
feet up on the stool in front. When anybody's there, I
sit on one of the seats of the club fender so that I can jump
up and down easily. I can't relax when I'm receiving.
Nobody believes it, but it's the responsibility. And yet,
one of my great pleasures is people I like coming to
Avenue Marceau. Several times a week we have friends
in at drink time. It's all very casual and unfussy. In spite
of not being the kind of hostess who plans ahead and has
exquisite little tit-bits to eat, I must be good at creating
rather a special atmosphere, because the most different
kinds of people constantly come in and see us and seem to
enjoy it. Of course there's always plenty of drink. My
sister Didine (her real name is Adrienne) once said that
my home is really more a Saloon than a Salon.

If, at drink time at Avenue Marceau, we all get on well,
we go off to a bistro. So the good talk doesn't stop, and the
food is not my responsibility, it's the *patron's*. I get my
ration of responsibility at work.

If, on the other hand, I see Paul-Emile get restless
during drinks I say, "Now children I am afraid you must
go, because we have a dinner and we must change."

As soon as I've got them out of the house, the maid
wheels in the dinner. This is a trick I learned from a
millionairess who entertained me in Chicago.

She wanted to get rid of the 'drinks' lot so that we could
dine, and her line was, "Now folks, I'm afraid you must
go as we're having soufflé for dinner."

Everybody was so impressed that in five minutes the

decks were cleared. Actually we started dinner with anchovies on toast!

Many of the people who come to see us belong to the theatre. They know we love them, that the atmosphere will be casual and that they won't be on show.

"You may like the theatre," I am constantly asked, "but why are your friends almost exclusively amongst the famous?" Here we go. The old question forever coming up.

Answer: I love success. This is a basic ingredient of my character. I believe success is no accident. It requires that little extra something that the ordinary run of people haven't got: that additional quota of beauty, courage, concentration, determination, energy, hard work, talent . . . all right yes—and luck too. All this dazzles me.

One of our principles is never, never to say, "Come and meet Noël Coward or Lena Horne or Marlene Dietrich."

We want our theatre friends to relax; not to have to 'sing for their supper'. Civilians, as Marlene calls them, are so tactless. When they meet show people in private they bombard them with terrible questions. Some get them into a corner and tell them how they adore them and that they've made a difference to their whole lives, which is a bore. Others are rude.

They say things like, "I thought you were terrible in that last film. You're not used to people telling you the truth, are you?"

So when theatre people come to see us we are very fussy about who comes in.

And everyone says, "*Quels snobs* the Seidmanns. We're not good enough to be invited with their *vedettes*."

I love star quality more than anything. I know I keep on about it, but I'll never get used to it. Hugh Beaumont, Binkie, the English producer who has been dealing with the theatre all his life, feels the same way. He'll never be blasé about star quality. Not that we don't often get infuriated. They can be impossible, the gold dust boys and girls. I've seen Binkie go white with rage and his blue eyes go steely grey at one of their temperamental tantrums. But three days after, he rings me from London and says, "I've laughed. I've got over it."

"I understand," I say. "Think of them standing alone backstage that minute before they go on, with the empty stage and 2,000 people in the house ready to tear them to pieces. And their not disappointing us. It makes up for a lot."

I keep my paperclips on my desk in a silver Fabergé cigarette case Binkie Beaumont gave me. I don't smoke. I never have. Binkie meant me to use it as a powder compact for my bag. But I love paperclips and taking them out of a silver case makes it glamorous. I like glamour to be an everyday thing—not for best. That's why I've just bought myself a sable coat, which is a madness. I wear it the whole time. Binkie is furious with me for having been so extravagant. But I cannot resist furs. I'd give a polite thank you for a diamond bracelet, but furs, that's something else again.

Neither Paul-Emile nor I can stand being bored for one single minute. Paul-Emile goes green when he's bored. People think he's going to faint, but I know it's only because he's bored. We're not bored by the same things, Paul-Emile and I. He's bored by musicals except *West Side Story* and *Fiddler on the Roof*. He's fascinated, in fact he's obsessed, by Scandinavia and Ingmar Bergman the Swedish film director. Ingmar Bergman and Brecht are the opposite of my cup of tea. All that misery.

Another big difference of opinion between Paul-Emile and me is maps. Paul-Emile has a passion for maps. A spot on a map meaning a town, a brown smudge meaning mountains, they're a source of dreams for him. I can only look at a map after I have been to a place and the spot has acquired a face and life and memories. Sometimes the memories are so poignant that I have to wait for years before I can bear to look at the spot on the map.

One thing the two Seidmanns have in common is our

love for the theatre, and we'd rather go to the theatre with each other than with anybody else. We go a great deal. It may sound childish (I never know why some things are considered childish, some not), but both Paul-Emile and I are grateful to be living in the age of Laurence Olivier. We are completely lifted out of ourselves, out of everyday life, out of the daily problems of existence by an Olivier performance. We love him so, off the stage as well as on.

My flat is full of beautiful furniture left me by an aunt, Auntie Lily, who was really my cousin. Gentle, pretty, she loved to laugh. She cried real tears when she laughed. She lived in Paris and was married to 'Uncle' Jackie, who had a beard and smoked cigars. They had no children. We three Spaniers were their children: I Ginette, the eldest, my real name is Jenny; Didine; and Janine the youngest. We'd have done anything to make Auntie Lily laugh. We loved making Mother laugh too.

I don't deserve all that beautiful furniture. I don't appreciate it, although I realize it fits in very well with my large apartment and the high ceilings and the mouldings and the rest of the antique jazz. Right through my youth I heard conversations about antique furniture: my Uncle Charlie stroking the legs of a chair and saying: "It can't be Louis XVI, it must be Directoire." On and on. It bored me then and it bores me now. But for Didine it was fascinating, and she became an interior decorator.

My bedroom is my favourite room in the flat. I am a bedsitter girl. I like my bedroom to contain my whole little private world: my bed, my desk, my gramophone, my radio, my typewriter, my files. My bedroom has little in common with Madame de Pompadour's boudoir. Fluffy it isn't. It used to be rather a mess, but now it's been done over completely. I waited a long time to have the bedroom I wanted. I preferred to wait and have it really good than just half-way. I am hopeless at decorating. A shutter closes down in my brain when the question crops up. (The same thing happens when people mention card games. The thought of a spade or a heart when it's on a playing card sends me round the bend.)

I interviewed many decorators for my room. The final test was my desk. My desk is an object of controversy. It is an office desk, green metal with drawers that slide in and out at a touch. All my friends scream with horror when they see the desk in my bedroom. They get quite red in the face with anger. I wish they'd mind their own business. *I* don't care if they have the Albert Memorial in the middle of their bedrooms. To me, my desk is an objet of necessity.

When decorators came into my room and said, "Beautiful proportions, lovely mouldings. We must, of course, get rid of the desk and put that exquisite little Louis XVI chest of drawers between the windows," they were *out*. They never knew what hit them. They just found themselves standing bewildered on the DR. P-E. S. mat outside the front door.

I admit I'm not a present for a decorator. What I really need is a decorator who specializes in hotels. I could easily live in a hotel. I love luxury hotels more than most things. Sordid hotels are my worst nightmare: the dread of having to end my days all alone in a dirty, sordid hotel haunts me. I know it's ridiculous, but there are whole streets I avoid just for this reason. To me a weekend in a lovely hotel is like a long holiday. From the moment the doorman takes my luggage from the taxi, my nerves smooth out. I get up to my room. I put on all the lights. I can make a hotel room into a home in under ten minutes. Then, like Kay Thompson's character 'Eloïse', I ring Room Service. There is no greater luxury than room service and a scotch and soda with enormous lumps of ice sipped all by oneself in a lovely clean, comfortable hotel room. My dream is the Savoy. That little corner suite where you get a glimpse of the Thames and a view of Waterloo Bridge. That view turns my heart over with love.

Tipping in hotels is a problem. I keep worrying about

doing the right thing. Some hotels make you feel small whatever you do. The Savoy makes you feel you always do the right thing whatever it is you do. All women over-tip. It's lack of confidence. I overtip, but there remains that lingering feeling that perhaps it still isn't enough. I'd like someone to write a handbook on tipping. It would make travelling a real pleasure for women: London-Claridges-head porter. . . .

There are some 'musts' in hotels. The most important are: never an inch of velvet and lots of free Kleenex. I despise hotels where there is no free Kleenex, and I have only to see an inch of velvet in a hotel and I can't wait to be out. Little pads for notes are important and stacks of thickly embossed writing paper. There must never be a ring on a piece of furniture where a glass had stood. That, like velvet, gives me the willies. Glossy sheets are impor-tant. And lots of towels. The biggest towels I have ever come across are at the Cumberland Hotel in London.

Head waiters, strangely enough, have never been a problem in my life. Even when I was quite young, for no apparent reason, they swept me to the best table with a flourish. Garson Kanin in one of his plays makes a character say, "Where you sit's everything in life." Exaggerated perhaps, but there's something in it. It's awful how one despises a man who takes you out and you don't get a good table and perfect service. I am grateful to all those dear *maître d'hôtels* who, over the years, have seen me to the best and most glamorous tables in London, Paris and New York.

In spite of all the fuss I make, I love my home. I travel a great deal and I love settling back there. I love the quiet bits: reading and mending and tidying and knitting. And I love it when my friends from all over the world ring up and come round. I will *not* have anyone coming in without ringing up first.

People have a way of bringing other people to Avenue Marceau. For instance, Danny Kaye brought us Maurice Chevalier, Lena Horne, Claudette Colbert; Richard

Avedon brought us James Baldwin, the negro writer. Dick Avedon is the great American fashion photographer, a special friend, a genius dragonfly. His first trip to Paris, as a young beginner, to photograph the Collections for *Harper's Bazaar* coincided with my first season at Balmain's, so we have known each other for over twenty years. We tend, in each other's company, to get rather overstimulated and excited.

One day, Dick rang me and said, "Will you do something for me?"

"Of course," I answered.

"Will you hide James Baldwin for a night or two?"

"Of course," I answered.

I had no idea what I was hiding James Baldwin from. It appeared that Dick Avedon and James Baldwin were supposed to do a book together, and Baldwin had to have two nights of peace to get it going, away from the television, the radio, the newspapers who were pursuing him in Paris. So, late that evening, James Baldwin arrived, armed with his typewriter and his toothbrush. We talked and then he went off to the spare room where, apparently, he worked half the night. I lent him a pair of my pyjamas. When I left for work next morning, he was asleep. The same thing happened next day, and when I came home from work, I found a very sweet little note of goodbye from James Baldwin. I've never seen him since. The book was finally done, and Dick Avedon and James Baldwin sent me, framed, for Christmas, the first page of manuscript written in Baldwin's hand in my spare room.

Noël Coward was staying with us once and reading the proofs of a book.

"You must read this," Noël said. "It's very amusing. Nancy's autobiography. Dedicated to me."

"Nancy who?" I asked.

"Nancy Spain," Noël answered.

"I've never heard of her," I said to Noël.

He couldn't believe it. I vaguely remembered . . .

pictures of a girl in a sweater on the front of buses in London, advertising Basildon Bond writing paper, I think.

"Tough. A duck. Is mad about Lord Beaverbrook and me," was Noël's brief description.

To Nancy Spain some months before, he had said, "You don't know Ginette Spanier? We all stay with her when we go to Paris. Marlene, me, the Oliviers."

The next time Nancy Spain came to Paris, with her journalist's passion for possible news, she thought she'd investigate this unknown Spanier woman. She found it extraordinary that she had never heard about me, although so many famous theatricals knew me well enough to stay with me.

So she came to lunch.

In my sitting-room when I rushed in late I saw a young woman in a navy suit looking up from a book. One of my books, from one of my shelves. Soft eyes. Shy. Why had Noël said she was tough, I thought. How often in the years that followed was I to see Nancy Spain look up from a book to greet me, at airports, in restaurants. . . . Nancy even read at traffic lights waiting for the red to turn green.

We laughed right through lunch.

I said, "Come and see the Collection, the Balmain dress show."

"The collection? Me?" Nancy queried.

"It's a terribly funny world," I said.

We walked down the short street, down the rue Magellan, down the rue François Ier, past the 'Belle Féfé', talking, talking, laughing. We had each found a friend. The quicksilver brain, the instant understanding, the sense of humour, the biting wit, they never lost their fascination for me.

At Balmain's, she roared with laughter.

"But it's a great story!" she exclaimed.

How often in the years to come was I to see Nancy's eyes light up and hear her say, "It's a great story!"

"I told you," I said. "It's all yours. Write it."

But she made *me* write it. That was later.

4

The Factory

To reach my particular kingdom at Balmain's I have to
pass through the boutique on the ground floor. The
boutique did not exist when I went to work for Pierre
Balmain in 1947. He engaged me to create it—from
scratch. The fact of my having worked as a sales-girl in a
gift department in Piccadilly in the thirties was supposed
to have fitted me for the job. Just about as fitting as riding
a bicycle being the right training for flying a jet! Actually,
it probably is, basically. In all jobs the pace may differ, but
the basic principles remain absolute.

I am constantly asked, "What is the secret of your
success?"

"Work and tidiness," is my answer. And I add, "When
we were small our mother taught us to count the dirty
linen before it went to the laundry and to count it again

when it came back clean. I think I can attribute my success, such as it is, to this simple principle as much as to anything else." This isn't the answer people want. They want a magic formula. The same sort of idea as the love philtre Isolde swallowed. A success philtre. But somehow in my career I've never managed short cuts. It's been work, work, work. Not that I'm complaining. I happen to like work.

The boutique was called 'The Kiosk' in my day and was a counter in a corner. We did enormous business that first season with a small black neckerchief on which were sewn five rows of pearls and a black sweater studded with diamonds. Once the boutique was successfully launched, Pierre Balmain switched me over to running the Couture.

Every day as I walk through the boutique, after the usual '*bonjours*', I am subjected to a typically French barrage of "Madame looks tired," "Madame doesn't look tired," "*Madame est bien coiffée,*" "Madame isn't *bien coiffée,*" and I walk up the stairs. That's when the heat hits me. It's like suddenly bumping into the tropics. I'll never quite get used to the heat. Sometimes when I write at my desk, my hand sticks to the paper. And I keep taking off my pearls. Pearls are terribly hot. I always wear pearls: either two big fat rows—costume jewellery—or three rows of beautiful cultured pearls. Those three rows have been growing in size and quality over the years. They're not yet nearly as big as I would like. Small jewels don't interest me. I love them big and, lets face it, showy.

I suppose the heat comes from all those lights everywhere and all that carpet and all those people and rarely a window open. Periodically, in a half-hearted way, I go over and open the window a crack. This habit of mine has earned me the name of the 'English governess of the Haute Couture'.

In the salon whilst we show the Collection, we have a semblance of air conditioning, but not the American type of icy blast. This has never caught on in France, and I share the French point of view. When I'm in America I find it difficult to get used to air conditioning. It just means I'm frozen in the heat instead of in the cold. As for the Maison Balmain, not to have it everywhere is, I think, a blessing in disguise. A very hot disguise. An atmosphere of sexiness is indispensable to Haute Couture. It lulls the powers of resistance. A healthy, brisk, cool temperature—no good at all. Anyone can resist inside a Frigidaire. But, overheated, airless, scent-laden, with ladies fainting occasionally, that's the formula. The strangest things are sexy in the couture. Fringe on a dress, for instance. Don't ask me why. Of deep, psychological significance, I suppose. But few women can resist a dress with a bit of fringe on it, especially on the hem with the leg showing through as she walks. Once we had a dress done up at the back with a large hook and eye. The hook and eye were embroidered the same colour as the dress and were hardly noticeable, but at the rehearsal of the collection, when I saw it for the first time, I said to Pierre Balmain, "That dress is going to sell because of the hook."

He thought I was mad. But I knew it was sexy, and I was right; the dress sold like hot cakes.

Pleating is good too and mink, of course. That dark mink called 'Dark'. Dark, dark brown which is almost black but just isn't. Much sexier than real, true black. Try and explain that. Chinchilla and light-coloured mink are not nearly as sexy; they're just expensive and luxurious. Sable is very, very sexy. Soft and dark, very soft and the weight of a feather.

My desk is at the top of the stairs right in the middle of everything. I like to know exactly what's going on in the area of my responsibility.

At intervals throughout the years interviewers say to me, "I don't quite understand what it is you do exactly at Balmain's."

I find it very difficult to explain it to them, although I did try to give a detailed picture of my duties in my first

book *It Isn't All Mink.* I don't have a thing to do with the
designing. Pierre Balmain does that entirely, but, in a sentence, I am responsible for a customer from the moment
she walks up the stairs to the moment her dress is delivered.
I don't personally sew, sell, fit, deliver, but I participate
constantly. I organize and I co-ordinate. One thing is certain: if anything, however small, goes wrong, I am called,
but quick.

The daily, the weekly, the monthly, the yearly 'figures'
are my especial care, and in this I am supported, helped,
encouraged by our two commercial directors. One must
not lose sight of the fact that a Maison de Couture, however Haute, is nearer the factory than the art gallery. The
number one importance is, of course, the creative beauty
of the clothes, but a very close second is the healthy
administration of the business.

Every single order that is taken in the Couture part of
Balmain's has to be signed by me. Strangely enough, I am
not really good at arithmetic. For instance, I refuse to
accept the new franc which has been in existence for the
last ten years; I am too old to adapt myself to such nonsense. And my knowledge of higher mathematics is
limited to adding, in English and on my fingers, and to
being able to deduct 10 per cent, the whole peppered
with a little guesswork. But I continually have to work out
long lists of complicated prices, and when these are checked
by the director, who won't allow a leeway of threepence,
I'm usually dead on the nose.

Luck and instinct and good hard sense are a great help to
me in life. I rely on them completely.

When I am working on a big order with a saleswoman
I am outwardly calm but I seethe inside with excitement.
I work with a speed which surprises even me. I sweep
everybody and everything out of my path and out of my
mind until the order is triumphantly signed. Then I
collapse with the most terrible indigestion.

The excitement of orders big or small never palls. Only

once was I beaten at the post in the way of speed—by Sophia Loren. Very humiliating. We dressed her for the film *The Millionairess* with Peter Sellers, which necessitated lists of dresses, coats, hats, bags, gloves, shoes, jewels. Loren and I would compile these lists together, and often she got there first. Actresses aren't usually like that.

My greatest friend in France is Claude Wittelson, the director of furs at Balmain's. Claude was already working marvels for Pierre Balmain when I appeared on the scene, so we've known each other a long time. He has humour, a love of the good things of life (and that includes good food and good drink), and a passion for the principles of liberty. In all the years we've worked together, in gaiety and depression, he has never failed me. He restores my sense of humour and my sense of proportion when I lose them. The thing which makes me lose my sense of proportion most is bad manners.

It's strange, I don't make friends all that easily in France. I have, of course, many wonderful French friends, but our intimacy has grown over the years—not love at first sight like in England and America. I suppose it's that French and English reactions to almost everything are fundamentally different, and I have remained very English in spite of my French looks. The other day at a party I met a French actor, Grégoire Aslan. I'd seen him in films and plays for years. We got on marvellously at once.

"You see," I said to myself, "you *can* make French friends just like that in a flash."

Grégoire and his wife Anne came to drinks at Avenue Marceau the next day. It turned out that his mother comes from Manchester and that Anne is 100 per cent English— and a Quaker into the bargain.

At Balmain's, close to my desk as you come up the stairs, is the hat department. This has nothing to do with me, which is a good thing. I am not a hat girl. When my hair is a mess, I wear a hat for camouflage. And that's as far as I go with hats. Except mink hats in winter. I suppose next winter it will be sable—how exciting. In literature, hats are supposed to do a great deal for a girl's morale. When she is depressed or has problems the author sends her out to get herself a new hat, and she feels a lot better. I prefer to go and have a *coup de peigne* or a Scotch and soda. I have the feeling that nowadays quite a lot of women feel like I do. Alas, poor *modistes*!

Hats have always been a problem for me. I remember a hat problem in my young days. Well, I don't quite remember. I remember so little about whole hunks of my life. My sister Didine and my girl friend Anne Salmon remember every single thing about my youth and tell me about it. Sometimes I cannot believe the things they tell me about me. Anne tells me that once I was invited to the country to a grand house party. (This was when I lived in England.) Apparently I went to buy myself a country hat so as to be terribly English—the Spaniers never lost a touch of Frenchiness through all their years in England. This house-party invitation must have come during my Irish Guards epoch, when I used to go and lunch at St. James's Palace with my friends 'on guard'. All that famous regimental silver; and the port going round in a strange, terribly important direction; and one of the officers, usually the youngest looking too beautiful in full uniform, getting up rather self-consciously in the middle of the meal to go and inspect things. To go back to my buying a country hat—it seems I went to a shop in Bond Street and came back with a white satin number. My instinct must have told me that there was something not quite right about white satin in the country, but apparently the saleswoman said, "Margaret Whigham got one exactly like this and she often goes to the country."

I may be the greatest saleswoman in the world but I've always been a lousy buyer. That's why, contrary to most women, I never go shopping.

All this was before Anne married Julian Salmon. His family own Lyons, and Julian and I were friends even

In my sister Adrienne's flat in London. Over my right shoulder is
a sketch of me by Clemence Dane

(*above*) Our favourite picture of our parents, on the terrace of our home in Finchley Road. (*below left*) Our beloved Deedee. (*below right*) Ginette and Didine

before he knew Anne. I remember that Julian, like all the Lyons heirs, went and worked in the kitchens of the Trocadero Restaurant as soon as he left university. When at night he was through with his stint of duty, he would dash out of the kitchens of the Trocadero, put on tails and take us out to places like the Midnight Follies.

As Julian said to me only a little while ago, "It was even easier when I was doing my waiter stint because I didn't even have to change. I was ready to go."

Then Julian married Anne who was my dearest girl friend, and the three of us have always had a beautiful time together. Not a cloud in all these years. We've laughed a great deal, and, oh, how we've talked!

In the old days Anne and I never drank alcohol. I used to get drunk on a cup of coffee. We were very cheap to take out and terribly good value. We were so enchanted with life.

I always loved clothes. I suppose it was my French upbringing. There is nothing casual about the French attitude to women's clothes; it is one of the important facts of life. Born in Paris of a French mother I quite naturally absorbed this point of view at the time of my first toddle in the Parc Monceau, that sinister park supposed to be so lovely, sitting there in the middle of the 17th Arrondissement where I was born. I remember that even when we were children there was a terrible fuss made over what we looked like, what we wore each time we went out to have tea with our little friends or when we were called into the drawing-room to be shown off to the grown-ups on Mother's 'at home' days. This attitude seemed quite normal to us.

When I grew older I longed for really good clothes. At the theatre, from my seat in the pit, I would gaze longingly at Gertrude Lawrence, who was always dressed by Molyneux, at Yvonne Printemps dressed by Lanvin. My dream was, one day, to have just one dress from either of those two famous couturiers. Now, I am dressed entirely

D

by Pierre Balmain. The best fitters, the best workmanship
—always. No wonder so many women are bitchy to me.
Jealous of my Balmain clothes.

The importance of expensive clothes is psychological as
well as everything else. Woman is not a symmetrical
animal. Nobody, but nobody, is identical both sides. I
don't mean back and front. Every woman is desperately
conscious of her own particular differences, and this is
what shakes her confidence in herself, even though the
betting is that few people are aware of, or care about, these
slight discrepancies. To have both sides fitted, as in custom-
made clothes (opposed to ready-to-wear—which are cut
in large piles with both sides, obviously, as alike as two
peas) does more for a woman's morale than even jewels.
Hence the continued existence of the Haute Couture. As
long as there are women with enough money to have both
sides fitted, we'll stay in business.

Ours is a weird world. Perfection is our law, our
unquestioned, immutable rule, its unrelenting demands
accepted by everyone from the smallest apprentice to the
most beautiful mannequin.

How is the very top standard in every detail of our business achieved? By hard, exhausting work from each and
every one of us, and a disregard of the normal rules
governing a commercial enterprise.

The apparent waste of both time and the materials of
our stock-in-trade is astonishing to anyone outside our
profession. Priceless stuffs are cut into with inches, almost
yards to spare. Should a dart be found wanting, the whole
front of the dress is cut again. Hours are spent, sometimes
late into the night, on the sewing of the lining of a gar-
ment. Every bead of an elaborate embroidery is sewn on
by hand. We worry endlessly over matching colours: for
the lining of a jacket, the underslip of a dress, the exact
shade of white to go with the pattern of a tweed. Long
technical discussions take place over the precise angle of a
découpe. Our eyes are so trained that a difference of a

millimetre is a matter of life and death to us. None of us ever queries these exaggerations or finds them strange. As I said, perfection is our law.

The result is *Haute Couture*.

I am often asked, "How does one go about it if one wants to buy a dress at Balmain's?" Here is the blow-by-blow saga of such an adventure.

For a start, the potential customer has to get admitted into our House. This is not as simple as it sounds. We, the creators of fashion, are ever on the lookout for copyists, the pirates of the Paris dress trade, and we try and make it as difficult as possible for them to come in and steal our ideas. Therefore, an unknown customer has to have an invitation before she is allowed to cross our threshold. The easiest way to achieve this is to be recommended to us by someone who is already one of our customers. Madame Potential Customer rings us up, says, "I am a friend of your client, Madame So-and-So, and I want to come and see the Collection on such and such a day."

An invitation is sent to her with the name of the *vendeuse* who looks after her 'sponsor' stamped in red ink on the top left-hand corner.

Armed with her precious invitation card, at three o'clock in the afternoon of the day in question, Madame Potential Customer comes up the stairs at Balmain's and gives her name to the receptionist whose table bars the entrance at the top. From then on, it is plain sailing: the receptionist calls out the name of the *vendeuse*, who, smiling amiably, detaches herself from the group of black-robed ladies hovering behind the receptionist's desk. The customer is then seen to her seat in the salon with all the honours due to her rank. If her mink coat is of good quality and her solitaire diamond large, a buzz of excitement will follow her entrance. "*Elle est très bien!*" you hear.

A little card is given to each customer as she comes into the salon. On it she notes the numbers of the models which catch her fancy. As the models pass on the runway, the name and number of each is droned out in French and English by one of the *secondes vendeuses* (the assistants to the *premières vendeuses*) in a long, monotonous litany.

"*Numero trente-trois*, number thirty-three, *Versailles*." (The double numbers like thirty-three, forty-four, sixty-six usually mean that Monsieur Balmain, as he christens them, likes them particularly.) The job of 'announcing the collection' is taken in turns daily by the *secondes vendeuses*.

Around three o'clock I say, "Who is announcing today? Are the model girls ready?"

At five minutes past three, I say, "O.K. *On y va!*"

This goes for every day with the exception of the first two shows of every season when it is tradition that I announce the Collection. On those two vital occasions, in spite of my efforts to keep calm, a certain edge of hysteria is inclined to creep into my voice as, backstage, around me, all hell is let loose. In *It Isn't All Mink* I have described the rush, the excitement, the tears, the wildness of an opening collection. I imagine very much the same atmosphere must reign by the stage manager's desk at the side of the stage on the first night of a musical.

I shall never get used to the emotion and the breathless anxiety of those opening shows, even though I have been part of this ceremony over forty times to date. That is the reason I am still in the Couture after twenty years of exhaustion. But Pierre Balmain and I feel we are getting old because we scream at everybody so much less than we used to!

To go back to the new customer looking at the Collection . . . at the end, after the bride has 'passed' (every Collection in Paris ends with the bride), the *vendeuse* will be waiting as her customer comes out of the salon, either to take her into a fitting room right away so that she can make her choice (we love that) or to fix an appointment for her to come back and make her choice at a later date.

In the fitting room, the customer gives the card on which she has listed her favourite models, and the *seconde vendeuse* brings them back over her arm in an untidy heap and dumps them down, often on the floor—our lovely models which only a few minutes before were parading royally on our beautiful mannequins.

If Madame Customer is very thin she can actually slip into the models made for our wraithlike mannequins and look at herself from every angle in the big mirrors which surround her. This makes the choice much easier, but it is very rare. Ninety-nine times out of a hundred, the dresses have to be placed in front of the customer, her two arms in the sleeves, the *vendeuse* pulling here and there so that Madame gets an idea of what the model will look like on her when it is made to her measurements. All this requires infinite patience and tact on the part of the *vendeuse*.

Sometimes, miraculously, a customer decides what she wants there and then. But mostly, the customer comes back once, twice or six times before she can make up her mind. You can't blame her when you think of the sums of money involved and especially as, almost always, the ladies will have to justify the expense incurred to the gentlemen in their lives. There may be terrible disadvantages in working for one's living—getting up in the morning, for instance, and, when one goes away for the weekend, not being able to stay on an extra day—but all this weighs for nothing against the horror it must be to have to ask a man for money when you want anything. Financial independence—the ultimate blessing.

When once the customer has chosen her dress or dresses and the final figures are agreed upon, the order is signed, the lady's measurements are taken by one of the famous fitters of the house, and the times of fittings are assigned. Then things follow the normal course of all fittings, with all the anguish contained in that innocent word 'normal'. During this stage of the operation the patience of the *vendeuse* is again put to a severe test, not to speak of the customer, who stands without moving for hours, as pins are put in and taken out.

At long last the dresses are ready, the labels sewn in (the last gesture before delivery); everything is packed in beautiful boxes stuffed with new, crackling tissue paper and delivered by a uniformed messenger with the initials P.B. on his cap.

Ultimately the order is paid for. We hope. . . .

So much for the unknown customer who comes into the shop. But every day there come up the stairs customers we have known for years, customers who came for the first time last season, customers who buy whole wardrobes, customers who buy one little dress, customers we love, customers we love less, and the great crowd of anonymous Balmain fans who come just for the show and whom we let in only after we are certain of their credentials. Between a hundred and three hundred people see the Collection every afternoon, and it is incredible the number of letters I receive from America and England which say, "Our visit to Balmain's was the highlight of our whole trip abroad."

A question I am often asked is, "Aren't you ashamed, in these days, to ask people to pay such fabulous prices for *frivolity?*"

I wonder whether people selling Rolls-Royces are attacked with this same rather tedious barrage. The luxury trade is not highway robbery. Every dress we sell is 'costed' as carefully, item by item, as the most mundane object sold in a supermarket. But quality *is* expensive to produce. I am not ashamed, I am proud to have a job selling the kind of merchandise I like and respect; a job which gives employment twelve months out of the year to 600 people (in my particular firm), and to many thousands more in subsidiary industries which depend on the Haute Couture.

Yet, after all these years of working for Pierre Balmain, I have never become completely Couture. I don't eat and breathe and sleep couture. And that goes for my own wardrobe as well.

My big numbers are well up to standard. But I tend to be slightly careless over little things—for instance, changing bags to go with an outfit—a nightmare when you are in a hurry. If you aim at being really well dressed, accessories are of primary importance. The slightest imperfection over shoe, glove, bag, and the whole image is shattered, just as a splintered windscreen hides from view the inside of the most luxurious car.

One day I was dashing down the rue François Ier past the 'Belle Ferronnière'. An American was sitting out in the sun having breakfast and shouted out to me, "Never again wear those shoes in town. You should be ashamed." It was James Hill, one of the gentlemen who married Rita Hayworth. I had met him the night before at the 'Cirque d'Hiver' with Burt Lancaster. They were making the film *Trapeze*. For hours we had sat with our hearts in our mouths whilst someone tried, over and over again, to do the triple somersault in the air from a trapeze high up in the roof on to the hands of someone hanging head down from another trapeze. I think the one hanging head down was Burt Lancaster. Then we all went out to dinner together to 'Le Père Louis' and ate *foie gras*.

I never wore those country shoes again in town, and I never saw James Hill again, either. He was very attractive. It's funny the people who have an influence on one's life, in a small or a big way. I like to think about it.

Ian Fleming once said to me, "You women make such a fuss about your clothes and you forget about your elbows." I've always remembered that remark and have tried to take care of my elbows ever since. Dear Ian Fleming.

Shoes are a thorny problem for me, of that there is no doubt. I freely admit that my shoes are not what can be called perfection. For some unknown reason, they come into the category of my meannesses. Everyone, however extravagant, draws the economy line somewhere. This is psychological; and to cross the psychological economy line is one of the most difficult feats in the world. For me, to get rid of shoes that don't actually let in the damp comes into that category. My shoes start off well enough; I get them from the expensive *bottier* down the street or from Marks and Spencer. But I don't get rid of them soon enough.

Another meanness of mine is the agony of throwing away soap. I collect the last thin slivers and stick them together, building a new multi-coloured cake of soap with them. This gives me enormous satisfaction and makes my husband feel quite ill. Vivien Leigh, who was wildly extravagant, felt like I do about soap. Good soap sticks very well; cheap soap crumbles as you try to squash it and has a tendency to stop up the basin. Soap squashing is not as easy as one thinks. Like everything in life, it requires technique.

People's psychological economy frontiers fascinate me. Take Lilli Palmer. She stops this side of chocolates with liqueur cherries inside. A slab of nut milk choc is O.K., but she draws the moral line at cherry liqueur chocolates. There is no extravagance she won't allow herself when it's a question of her glorious home high up in the Swiss Alps, but cherry liqueur chocolates—No.

Lilli is one of the people who take an interest in my make-up. Particularly my eye make-up . . . ah, there's the rub. I know I'm slapdash about it. If I forget the green, Lilli gives me hell. If I remember it, Noël Coward says I look like a parrot. It's a great problem. Marlene Dietrich finally solved it by bringing me the right stuff and standing over me until I learnt how to manage it. For practical salvation in any quandary, Marlene has no equal.

Making up your eyes is exciting because you never achieve it twice exactly alike. Nor both eyes. At least I can't, so I never know what I'll end up looking like. Noël Coward says I often look like a touring company *Madame Butterfly*.

5

A New Life

Paris couturiers are continually asked to go all over the
world to show their collections. Sometimes the jaunt is a
lightning one—weekend distance—and therefore does not
interfere with the daily showings in Paris. These are
sacred. On these 'lightning' trips the clothes are frenziedly
packed after the collection on Friday, the girls and the
habilleuses (the dressers) travel all night, show in Cannes or
Copenhagen on the Saturday, again on the Sunday and are
back in the fold by Monday morning. A weekend of
frenzied packing, unpacking, ironing, packing, unpacking,
ironing. And one must not imagine that such concentrated
work is a brake to the social side of the outing. The
girls probably don't go to bed for the three nights and
arrive back triumphant, if a bit weary, their arms full of
flowers. For weeks after one of these trips letters arrive

bearing the postage stamps of the countries they have visited.

At other times, the collection goes further afield: to America, Japan, South Africa. For these excursions the dresses are remade. As I said before, the Paris show is sacred. Pierre Balmain loves those long journeys. He usually takes two of our girls with him, the stars of the season, and finds local talent on the spot to complete the *cabine*. The *cabine* is the room where the mannequins dress, and live, and drink champagne and beer, and tell each other's fortunes. They share this small, overheated, over-crowded room with the *habilleuses*, from whom they hide nothing—but nothing—of their lives and griefs and joys and problems. We have three *habilleuses* and one *chef de cabine*, the head dresser, who is boss of that particular empire. *Cabine* does not only designate the room, it also means the ensemble of the mannequins, like "This year we have a very beautiful *cabine*," meaning a very beautiful group of model girls. When I started work at Pierre Balmain's I knew so little about the couture that, each time somebody said the word cabine, I thought they meant the lavatory.

In the autumn of 1956 La Maison Balmain was invited to take the Collection to the town of Chester for two big charity galas. I don't usually travel with the circus, but as it was England, *my* country, Balmain asked me to go with them. Mr. Leonard Harris of Brown's of Chester had done things on the grand scale: a chartered plane from Paris to Manchester, a Rolls-Royce to meet us there, press photo-graphers, television cameras. . . .

On the way there, we were all in the plane—Balmain, Erik Mortensen (Pierre Balmain's attractive Danish assis-tant—a great friend although he constantly bullies me about my accessories), six model girls, two dressers, the enormous baskets of clothes and myself—a theatrical com-pany on tour. It was very bumpy weather and, to take our minds off the rather rickety aspect of the enterprise, we read out our 'stars' in the paper. I remember mine were: "On no account travel today." Everybody laughed rather shakily.

The shows in Chester were a great success. We all fell in love with the bishop, and the girls bought more cashmere sweaters than can be worn in a normal lifetime. Then the circus took itself back to Paris, whilst I went to London for a few days. On the platform in Chester it was the first and only time in my life I have been seen on to a train by the station-master in his top hat. Most enjoyable.

In London I rang up Nancy Spain, and we had lunch together. I had not seen her since that first lunch in Paris. This time it was no shy girl in a navy suit who greeted me at Wheeler's Restaurant in Old Compton Street, the Spain headquarters. It was the other version: trousers, sheepskin coat, reading, of course. As Nancy got up to greet me, books seemed to spill off her. She kicked them under the table.

Her authority was breathtaking. The service she got, with the waiters skipping about grinning with pleasure! Again we laughed all through lunch. I described my Chester adventures. Nancy could not get over the fact of a whole couture collection going from Paris to Chester without even touching London.

"Why Chester?" she asked.

"Because they invited us," I answered.

"Why not London?"

"Because they didn't invite us."

"Too good to be true," Nancy said. "You must do it for the BBC."

She rushed to the telephone. Came back and said, "Come on."

One pound tip to the doorman, and I was bundled into a taxi. Before I could collect myself I was in front of a microphone in Broadcasting House being interviewed by the famous Nancy Spain. Lorna Pegram was the producer on that first, to me, fateful day. She remembers every detail, even that I was wearing a black and white plaid coat and that Nancy said to her, "Isn't it lovely? It's from Pierre Balmain. Try it on."

I did not know it, but at that moment a whole new, exciting secondary life was starting for Ginette Spanier, shop girl and *directrice*.

Ever since that day the microphone has never, never lost its magic for me.

After that, Nancy Spain came a great deal to Avenue Marceau. We had so much in common: surnames to start with—Spain and Spanier. Things we hated, like 'what people think', amateurs and laziness and antiques (although I do love old churches, Norman ones). Things we loved, like work and the heat of the sun and laughter and music halls. She brought great gusts of fresh air into my existence, great gusts of English air. Yes, amongst other things, Nancy brought me England, a side of England I'd never known before: for instance, I'd never been to a pub before meeting her. Also she was the opposite of a *bourgeoise*; Nancy Spain, and I loved that. I, on my side, brought Paris to Nancy, and she loved that.

Nancy was obsessed with the idea of Paris under the German occupation. She kept on asking me what it had been like, the streets, the atmosphere, she wanted to know everything, to visualize it all. Nancy hated the Germans as much as I did. Before meeting her, I had written, at the instigation of Josh Logan the American director, creator of *Mr. Roberts*, of *South Pacific* (to name only two of his successes), a day-to-day account of our four and a half years of being hunted. My friends had been very kind about it, and had made efforts to have it published. All the publishers, with kind little letters, had sent the manuscript straight back. I didn't want to show it to Nancy, because, everywhere she went, people bothered her with their manuscripts—she, the book critic of the *Daily Express*. But I was so bored with describing 'what it had been like during the occupation' that I said, "All right. Read it.

There isn't a detail left out. I've got no imagination. But for heaven's sake don't think I want you to do anything about it. I have no illusions. It's unpublishable."

Nancy read it. She was interested, but she agreed that it was unpublishable.

Nancy realized a whole lot of things about me: that the undiluted couture diet was beginning to pall, that I had always longed for the 'hammy' side of life and had never had the guts to do anything about it and that, quite apart from anything else, at the end of the month there wasn't all that amount of money in the kitty. So she decided that something had better be done about that manuscript after all. To start with, she thought she'd make me into a 'personality', if you'll excuse the expression. It suited me fine. She set to and wrote two full-page features about me in the *Daily Express*; one, me at work, Madame la Directrice; the other, at home giving a party. Over the years the very words Nancy Spain used in those pieces keep cropping up in articles about me all over the place.

This is when my friends started shaking their heads. "Cheap publicity," they muttered.

Clemence Dane said to my sister, "Do you think I should write to Ginette and condole?"

I, on the other hand, was delighted. I shall never get over the excitement of seeing my name in thick black print, the thicker, the blacker, the larger the better, even if what is written below is not all that complimentary.

As Nancy used to say, "Never forget that two days later, it wraps the fish. The only thing they'll remember is your name if it's in big enough print."

Nancy and I shared this vulgar streak. We unashamedly confessed to enjoying things like success and money and publicity. It was the 'unashamedly' I think which upset people.

Then came the burning question of the book. Nancy realized what was wrong with it. The readers had to be made interested in the woman who had lived through

those war years: she sent me home to write my youth.
My sheltered, lace-ruffled youth, as she called it. She said
this would be a good contrast to my fainting from hunger
in the street, and the misery of my life during the
Occupation.

So I sat in my bedroom and wrote about my youth.
Every free moment I had, I wrote about my youth. As a
matter of fact, from that day on, most of the spare
moments I've had I've sat in my bedroom writing. It is
one of my great joys.

When I gave my homework to Nancy Spain, she was
agreeably surprised. Suddenly she felt it might be good
enough to show to one of the big publishers. She took the
two manuscripts, my youth and the war, to Collins, and
they said, "Let's see the girl."

I couldn't believe it when Nancy rang me from London.
The thought that one day my name might be printed on
the outside of a real book. Too much.

I went over to London.

Nancy said, "Here she is."

"Write a third part—the Couture. Sandwich the war in
the middle. Cut the whole thing to normal proportions,
and you've got your book," they said.

"I thought the couture could be a second book," I murmured, to which Nancy replied quick and sharp:

"Try writing *one* book that sells." And then, "I'll help
you."

It Isn't All Mink was born.

We wanted to call it *Mink—the Hard Way*. But my
mother worried that people would think her daughter had
not led a blameless life in order to obtain her mink coat.
She belongs to a generation which considers 'that' way the
'hard' way. To me, working for a mink coat from nine to six
every day for over a quarter of a century, and paying for it
myself at the end is the harder way. However, not wanting
to spoil the general happiness of this world-shaking event—
a Spanier book—I gave in about the title. But down on

my contract with Collins I am 'hereinafter called the author' and the name of my masterpiece is *Mink—the Hard Way.*

Nancy and I had a lovely time hacking away at the book. I could not possibly have done it alone. How can one boil down one's own deathless prose to a concentrated quarter, throwing the other three-quarters into the dustbin? I needed Nancy Spain's ruthless shears.

Even now when I manage to cut a paragraph, a sentence, even a word out of what I am writing, I can feel her nudge me and say, "Good girl."

We also had the whole Couture to write from scratch.

It was very hard work fitting it all in between my Balmain responsibilities and Nancy's multiple commitments: her writing, her pieces for the *Daily Express* and for *She* magazine, her radio and television work, her personal appearances, not to speak of our separate home lives. But we thrived on work. It was lovely to have found someone with the same vitality and enthusiasm and energy that I had. I realize that my vitality and fierce powers of concentration must often be boring to live with, in spite of the fact that President Kennedy said, "I suppose if you had to choose one quality to have it would be vitality."

Nancy was unbelievably generous with her time, with her advice. She had set her heart on the book, and when Miss Spain set her heart on something—well. . . . But let it not be imagined that with it all she was an angel of tolerance. I remember remarks like, "Would it hurt you to write one sentence that will not make everybody feel physically sick?" and "The banality of your choice of words is such that it makes 'Peg's Paper' look like Marcel Proust." I would crumple up with laughter. There must be something about me which incites my nearest and dearest to flights of insulting oratory at my expense. Take Noël Coward, his imagery has yet to be equalled. But if I know they love me, and they're funny, they can say anything they like. I laugh and I usually act on their advice. If I know they don't love me, and there's acidity instead of humour in the statement, the slightest criticism makes me furious. How dare they?

Nancy Spain was the person out of all the world who made me laugh most—unexpectedly, from deep down inside me. She was a supreme story-teller. Her sagas were always based on a personal adventure, then lovingly nurtured, exaggerated, embellished with imitations, until they became great, hilarious masterpieces.

It was during our work together on *It Isn't All Mink* that I wrote the following piece about her:

She's brilliant, she's outrageous, she's madly extravagant, she's in love with the *Daily Express* and a little boy of five named Tommy. She does not always have the greatest tact in the world, she has a photographic memory, and the most beautiful hands any woman could dream of possessing. She is brash, she is shy, she is impatient, she has a glorious sense of humour. She knows the words of every song that light music has produced in England these last thirty years, she is generous in the grand manner without thought of self or tomorrow, she is brutally outspoken. She changes her shirt three times a day. She has a deep sentimental passion for London, she is short-sighted, she loves the records of Fats Waller, champagne, Veganin, Felsol, oysters, Wheelers, music-hall comedians. She has one of the sexiest voices on the BBC, she overtips wildly, she has played most games superlatively well, she can write lyrically, beautifully, sensitively. She can write vulgarly, hurtfully. She has her own brand of chic, she refuses boredom unless she is paid for it, she is detested implacably by the Nobs. The people love her, have made her into a public figure and acclaim her as she passes in the street in her big white car.

The Bathroom. Of this room Nancy Spain wrote: "The bath-room is a reflection of the sitting-room at its wildest. Here, caught like flies in amber on the walls, are the signed photographs of the people you have just left shouting in the sitting-room. The walls are wild with talent."

Paul-Emile in Brittany, on the River Odet. Paul-Emile loves
Brittany almost as much as he loves Norway

With Dickie Henderson, the comedian, and Nancy Spain at The
National Town Criers Championship in Hastings. We'd just
chosen the winner

6

Hereinafter Called the Author

One day in Paris I received a telegram; "*You're lunching with Christina Foyle Friday 1 o'clock Ivy so shut up.*"

This was a parody of a telegram Noël Coward had sent Paul-Emile and me years before saying: "*You're spending Christmas in Jamaica so shut up.*"

I rushed across the Channel, and at that lunch Nancy and I sold Christina Foyle the idea of featuring *It Isn't All Mink* at one of her famous literary luncheons. She hadn't even read the book. How could she? No final copy existed. Only about ten different typescripts, over which Collins were still dickering.

But Christina Foyle having agreed to give one of her Dorchester luncheons for me did the trick! Collins were so impressed—there are only ten Foyles lunches a year, and about 30,000 books are published—that they decided on immediate publication.

Hereinafter I was really called the author.

I had never believed it would happen. That one day my life would be sandwiched between the two hard covers of a book. But it was coming true. What is more Collins suggested a preface by Noël Coward.

Since 1924 when I'd seen *The Vortex* for the first time at the Everyman Theatre, Hampstead (a converted drill hall next to where we lived), I'd been an avowed, unashamed, adoring Coward fan. It had taken me twenty years to meet him, and the friendship that had grown between us was—still is—one of the things I am proud of. Noël had encouraged my book when it was in its war form, and through the years we'd laughed and talked and spent many, many marvellous hours together. But could one presume on friendship so far as to get Noël Coward to endorse my book with his signature? I wrote to him saying, "Please don't if you don't want to." Three days later the preface arrived.

Nancy Spain had made a shop girl into an author, had got the name Ginette Spanier printed on the outside of a book with a preface by Noël Coward, but that wasn't enough for her: she wanted the book to sell. Not only for my sake, but also for Collins who had gambled on me 'blind'. Those books had to be moved off the warehouse shelves.

Nancy who had studied every aspect of the book business, explained to me the three important stages which bring a book from warehouse to reader.

Firstly, the publisher's traveller. He carts around endless numbers of books every day to sell them to shops and bookstalls, and could not care less which of them succeeds. Somehow we had to persuade him, when he was on his rounds, to take my book out from amongst the others in his little suitcase and give it just that extra plug. So I got Collins to agree to my addressing their travellers at one of their sales conventions. I remember it was a boiling hot day. I dressed myself up to the nines and I enjoyed every minute of it. I was on my own ground there, a saleswoman these last twenty-nine years. I spoke as one of them, not as an author.

The next step was the bookseller. Hundreds of new books appear every week, and the bookseller could not care less which of them succeeds with his customers as long as he does his daily 'figures'. I had to get him interested in my book just a little more than in all those others. Persuade him to put it in the window of the shop, in a conspicuous place on the counter, on the front of the bookstalls. So, I started going around the important London bookshops, the important bookstalls like the one on Waterloo Station—selling my own wares, I, who for half a lifetime, had sold other people's.

Then we had to get the book from the bookstall to the reader. To create a demand for it, in other words. So, Nancy groomed me for television, for radio, for the lecture platform.

I rushed backwards and forwards across the Channel like a spinning shuttle between Haute Couture and the literary life.

And the excitement really started. It was all I had ever hoped for. Collins gave a party for me on publication day. There were interviews, photographs—a whole series of me on a motorbicycle—heaven knows why!—my mink coat flying out behind (as a point of interest I can't even drive a car!)

The Foyles luncheon at the Dorchester was a riot. Kenneth More was chairman and made a speech which was not only funny, but very sweet and generous to me. Nancy Spain proposed the vote of thanks. Paul-Emile came over. My family was there. For the first time in literary history we had a dress show at a literary function. I brought over from Paris two of our star mannequins, both

English girls. We showed only great, formal, glamorous evening gowns with tiaras. The 'girls' were Bronwen Pugh and Pat Donald Smith, now Viscountess Astor and Lady Selsdon respectively.

Most of the London couturiers turned up to hold my hand and cheer me on. I had to say a few words. Terrifying. But it went off all right.

Then the city of Chester, which had been the starting point of my new life, gave me a civic reception. A banquet in the town hall which was floodlit for the occasion. I sat between the bishop and the mayor. We all three made speeches. A Ginette in Chesterland evening. We still send each other Christmas cards, the bishop and I. It's easy for him, but every year I go through the My Grace, Your Grace, His Grace agony. I've skipped some years because of not being able to face the terrible hazard of how to address the beautiful Bishop of Chester.

I spoke at an 'authors tea' at Harrods, and the scene is photographed in my memory. My father had been very ill but made the effort to go just the same. There he sat, at at a table in front of me, tears pouring down his face as he saw his daughter on the platform and the audience applauding her. It was all I could do to keep from breaking down myself, he looked so happy and so proud—and suddenly so old. It was one of the last times he went out in public.

I was invited to broadcast and to appear on television. I followed Nancy Spain's instructions every inch of the way. I dreaded being a hopeless amateur. The first time I went on television—on the "Tonight" programme, Nancy said, "You've got absolutely no experience of television; so play it quietly. Listen carefully to the questions of the interviewer. Nobody ever does. It will endear you to the audience.

I would never have believed, as I trembled on the brink of my first television interview, that, some years later, the boss of that very programme, Cliff Michelmore, would come over to Paris with a television crew, specially to do a big programme on me: Ginette Spanier walking down the street of her 'village', Ginette Spanier at Balmain's, Ginette Spanier sitting talking in her apartment.

The second time I went on television, Nancy said, "Start it quiet again, but you can flash your teeth in the middle. Then go quiet again at the end."

The third time she said, "You're on your own. You can go mad if you like."

It was the day Derek Hart decided to be unkind to me. He warned me beforehand so I said, "Give me a whisky and soda."

He said, "You better take two."

I did. When he asked me, "With your passion for celebrities, Madame Spanier, who are you going after next? and how are you going to set about it?"

I answered, "I can't expect you to believe that I've never 'gone after' anybody in my life. They just fall from heaven. Now, tell me, Mr. Hart, if somebody were to ring at *your* door, would you bang it in his face just because his name happened to be Noël Coward?"

Next day there were letters in the newspapers saying "Bravo! at last somebody had answered back to one of those cruel interviewers." Dear Derek.

Since those early days, I have been asked to appear on many varied programmes; the most fascinating, I think, was a series of twelve religious discussions run by Anthony Hoyland when he was at TWW. The chairman was Professor Frank George who now has the chair of Cybernetics at Brunel College. The panel consisted of two Churchmen of different denominations and me. What I was doing in the midst of such learning, it is hard to comprehend, but I have great faith and I always say thank you to God as well as please. I believe deeply in prayer. My colleagues, were they Anglican, Roman Catholic or Baptist, were very kind to me, and the strange mixture we presented gave rise to a great deal of correspondence and interest. For me, it was an intoxicating experience intellectually.

At the time of the launching of *It Isn't All Mink*, another of my friends came into the picture: Ida Cook. Ida and her sister Louise are unique characters. Their interests are heterogeneous. Music, especially opera, is their great passion. They are intimates of Rosa Ponsell and Maria Callas, to name only two great singers who are among their friends.

Just before the war, though not Jewish themselves, they succeeded in getting twenty-nine Jewish people out of Germany under the noses of the Gestapo, and thus saved them from the gas chambers—veritable Scarlet Pimpernels. Ida has written their story called *We Followed Our Stars*. I bow very low as I mention the name of the Cook sisters. To add to the picture, Ida Cook, under the name of Mary Burchell, is a writer of light romance; and, up to date, has written 110 novels—110 stories with happy endings. What a rest in a world of violence and cruelty and misery!

Ida Cook lectures all over England and suggested I try doing the same thing to plug my book. I knew this was a whole way of life especially in America, although I wondered why anyone should prefer to go to a lecture rather than to a cinema or to the theatre. It seemed a weird form of entertainment. I was, however, willing to try my hand at it.

I'd always been rather a 'chatty' person—we all are in the family. We love stories and are quite good at making the most of the funny side of things. My sister Didine is one of the best story-tellers I know: she has total recall and peppers her anecdotes with imitations. I've always been her best audience. On the other hand I did know that 'talking' and 'speaking' were two very different things so it was with a certain amount of trepidation that I followed Ida Cook up some dark stairs in Newman Street to be interviewed by her lecture agent, Maurice Frost. We talked for a few minutes, and, before I knew where I was, Mr. Frost had booked a lecture tour for me in the North of England— my first lecture: Newcastle-upon-Tyne.

Straight to Nancy Spain I went for instructions on the technique of lecturing. Invaluable advice poured forth. And up to Newcastle we went: I, the Cook sisters and Nancy. My three Geordie friends (Nancy Spain was born in Newcastle-upon-Tyne and had lived there half her life) wanted to set me off on my new career in style. Little did we know how far this latest adventure of mine would take me, geographically at least.

My lecture was a success, and in the evening some Newcastle friends of the Cooks gave an uproarious party for me. Miss Spain got drunk and sang Geordie songs in dialect. I was launched.

(Incidentally, my sister Didine has since followed me on the lecture circuit and is a big hit wherever she goes.)

Nancy's book *My Boy Mo* had just come out, so we decided to make my lecture tour into a great bookselling offensive on the side. All over the North of England, we went into every bookshop we could find and hawked our masterpieces with gusto. And Nancy played golf. Nancy was in the middle of her golf obsession: the importance of pitting one's brain and the co-ordination of one's muscles against the lie of the terrain, the direction and the strength of the wind. Not my brain. Not my muscles. The athletic life is not for me. I just followed. So, during that tour, I not only learnt to speak, but I walked over acres of beautiful, green, carefully tended English grass into the bargain.

I was lucky: the ladies of the clubs at which I spoke were prejudiced in my favour because, alone among English lecturers, I came to them straight from Paris. They believed I would bring them a magic message, the secret of that highly publicized French sex appeal. Even now after ten years of speaking all over England and America, I am thankful to say this reputation for glamour still clings to me.

Nancy warned me, "Don't get too pleased with yourself. So far it's been all jam, but one day it will happen. You'll stand there on that platform and nobody will know you, nobody will care, they won't even have your name right and they won't react to one word you say. It happened to me when I was 'Woman of the Year'. It's the most ghastly experience in the world."

One morning, out from Manchester, Nancy was going to play golf with a boy-friend, and they dropped me off at Blackburn where I was speaking. A cold sooty rain was falling. The building at which I was deposited was anything but inviting and Nancy said, "Today's the day. What the hell can you talk to them about that will catch their attention? I know. Football. The Blackburn Rovers."

"May I ask what football has to do with the Haute Couture?" I said—rather superior.

"Stick to football," were Nancy's last words as she drove off, rattling her golf clubs.

I spoke in a kind of chapel—unlighted—a grey, sad light filtering through as the rain continued to fall outside.

A lady who had obviously been delegated to introduce me at the last minute and had only glanced at my brochure said, "It gives me great pleasure to introduce Mrs. Ballmain (Bal to rhyme with ball and main like on a horse) from the *Hot* Couture."

Not a soul smiled, and I had no friend in the audience to enjoy it with me.

In the front row I glimpsed two ladies with hearing aids, and two who were asleep. I got up boldly and pinned on a gay smile. I started. There was not the least response, just deadly silence. Nothing—but nothing.

I said to myself, "Nancy! This is it," and I started again: "Before I speak about *me* and the mad world I come from, please allow me to speak about *you* for a minute. On my way here I passed some great gates and I asked what they were. The answer was 'The home of Blackburn Rovers'."

The effect was magical. Dropped were the hearing aids,

the sleepers woke up with a start. "Can you imagine", I continued, "what it means to me who comes from Paris, actually to see the home of the Blackburn Rovers?"

The whole chapel cheered. I never looked back until the end of my talk. I was learning my trade, and I had become a Rovers' fan.

This story is no slight on my warm-hearted, dearly-loved Lancashire audiences. Throughout the years they have asked me back over and over again to that triangle which has Manchester in the south, Blackpool in the west and Clitheroe in the north, and they've always given me a beautiful welcome.

Golf was by no means Miss Spain's only interest. Great enthusiasms into which she threw herself headlong sweeping her friends along in her wake, would overwhelm her at intervals.

First and foremost, of course, there was journalism. As she wrote to me once, "My long troubled glorious impossible savage exciting exasperating love affair with the *Daily Express*."

Nancy Spain and Lord Beaverbrook were very close. They both suffered from asthma, so each understood what the other was going through. Nancy dined frequently at Arlington House. Her stories, adventures and outspoken opinions entertained Beaverbrook. The descriptions of their outsize discussions were marvellous. Nancy really loved the old man, and on every birthday she sent him the number of his years in red roses. Once, she was a rose short. Beaverbrook pointed it out at table, and in the middle of dinner Nancy sent out for another rose. The last time of all there were eighty-four roses in the bouquet.

Nancy read voraciously, and now and then a book would particularly take hold of her imagination. I remember the time of Mary Renault and *The King Must Die*. Hours of talking and speculating about ancient Greece and Theseus the King, and the Bull Dancers and Crete. I think *The King Must Die* had something to do with Nancy building a house on the Greek island of Skiathos.

Later, it was *The Queen's Necklace* by Frances Missiker, so we switched to the French Revolution.

And there was pop music. Nancy was right on to it from the start. I remember her excitement at the novelty of it all. She interviewed Larry Parnes, Tommy Steele, Adam Faith, the pioneers of this new way of life. We'd listen to the radio, and Nancy would analyse it, would explain it. She knew something big had hit us. She adored being on "Juke Box Jury".

At the beginning, I confess, I was rather bewildered, but, finally, I caught the bug and I still listen every night in bed to what used to be the Light Programme and now, for some unknown reason, calls itself Radio Two. At long last I even 'made' "Juke Box Jury" myself. That's where I met Lulu for the first time. She was the Mystery Guest, I remember. It was one of her first appearances in public, after her first hit. She was 14½. We met again the other day on the Pete Murray Show and reminisced, Lulu now a big star, the whole of twenty years of age. And one of the winners of the 1969 Eurovision Song Contest; Lulu, just as enchanting and gay as before, and newly married to a Bee Gee.

The beautiful Pete Murray, there is another one who has helped me consistently. He welcomes me on his show when I am in London, and recently we even did a show live from Paris.

I know I'm tiresome going on endlessly about people being beautiful. But I do love it so. I never get used to it. Each time I see Marlene Dietrich, and I see her very often, her beauty hits me anew. And so it is with all my friends who are good-looking. It gives me such pleasure. (I cannot write about Marlene Dietrich although I have much to say about her. But how can I compete with Hemingway, Noël Coward, Cocteau, Philippe Heriat, Kenneth Tynan and all those others who have laid the laurel wreaths ot their love and admiration at her feet? I will only say that I am proud and grateful to be her friend.)

On the other hand, I really hate people who look a mess. And if they look unwashed I get furious. Whatever their fancy dress, oh please, please, let them be clean!

In 1960, *It Isn't All Mink* was sold to America and the publishers invited me over to New York to change the book to suit the American market. I felt like "Champagne Goût Americain".

I had always wanted an excuse to go to New York. I'd been there twice and I have so many friends over there. I couldn't afford to go as a tourist, but I had hoped that one day the Maison Balmain would provide the solution. I had never dreamt that literature would be my magic carpet. I packed my bags and went, and from that day I have popped backwards and forwards across the Atlantic—once more the spinning shuttle.

In New York it was glorious. I appeared on dozens of television and radio programmes. I was constantly interviewed. In the United States interviewers have so much space in newspapers, so much time on television and radio, that it rather goes to one's head this being able to go on and on about oneself. Especially after England when you have to make your point and off in three minutes. But, then, in England you have to be more of a 'pro' to get away with it.

Interviews—whether for newspapers, television or radio —are occasions when you have to chase everything else from your mind, your concentration and your intelligence extended to its maximum. I can be tired, I can feel depressed, I can be under the weather, yet the very moment I am in front of a microphone life flows back into me.

And I kept rushing back to Paris to sell dresses.

My new life was full of thrills. I wrote a series of articles for the *News of the World*. I wrote a monthly column for an English magazine, a job which lasted more than four years.

I wrote several series for a Swedish magazine. My book was serialized in England, Australia, in *McCall's Magazine* in the U.S.A., in South Africa.

I was asked to do odd things like being one of the judges in a competition for the best town crier in England. I was the first woman ever to be interviewed live via Telstar. Satellites are old hat now, but this was the first big live news telecast from Paris to America by satellite. Amidst all those men on the programme I was the only woman, Heaven and CBS only know why! Quite a moment it was when, in the middle of unbelievable brou-ha-ha, with all the bigwigs of television—including William Paley himself, head of CBS Network—in the control room, over the loud-speaker boomed, "*Selence absolu trois minutes*". We knew we were waiting for a man-made satellite to be in exactly the right position in the sky, with the right side of its 'face' turned towards us. As one American technician had said to me, "She's a pain in the arse. There's only one side of her from which we can beam." Like an actress who only allows one side of her face to be photographed.

An hour later I got a cable saying, "Knew you'd be the first woman to talk in space. Lena." Lena Horne had seen and heard me in New York.

Then *It Isn't All Mink* was published in France. And was a terrible flop!

7

American Notebook

Whilst I was in the United States, Random House, my publishers, introduced me to an American a lecture agency. A lady rattling with beads auditioned me in my hotel bed-room, and I was booked for four dates, at a price which made my head reel. My first lecture was in Dearborn, Michigan. In those early days in England I had only ever spoken at luncheon clubs, cosy affairs with the audience warmed up by a little preliminary food. In Dearborn I was to speak in a cinema, and I was slightly taken aback when I was driven up to it and saw the size of the place. I insisted on being photographed under the canopy which sported the name Frank Sinatra in large letters. Ever since that first venture of mine in the American lecture field, the state of Michigan has been a staunch supporter of G. Spanier. To date I have spoken in fifteen towns in Michigan.

American audiences are different from English ones. The English look for entertainment. They want to laugh. The Americans want plenty of facts. They want to go away feeling they have learnt something.

Except for Paul-Emile, who knows what a gruelling adventure my American tours are, and actors such as Maurice Chevalier, and others who have had experience of one-night stands, few people take my lectures in the United States seriously. They don't realize what it's like. The Lunts do. They say things like, "Have you played Grand Rapids?" It's the word 'play' I enjoy. Whenever I lecture in a theatre where Maurice Chevalier has appeared, like the Fisher Theatre in Detroit, I send him a postcard. The fact that I do my act once, and at 11 o'clock in the morning, whilst he fills the Fisher Theatre night after night makes not the slightest difference to Maurice's respect.

"How many people have filled the Fisher Theatre even only once?" he says.

Jack Benny said, "You mean to say you go out there without scenery and without music and without a script, and in the morning when they're all stone cold sober? You must be nuts."

Some audiences are very difficult, mostly when they're rich, and there are lots of ladies with their little sables round their necks. Once I was in a rich club in St. Louis, Missouri, and I looked around and knew it was going to be tough.

"I must have a drink," I said to the secretary. She was horrified.

"You can't," she said, "this club is dry."

"Oh, it can't be," I answered. "But if I faint right now, down on the floor at your feet, won't you revive me with a little brandy?"

She was more and more horrified.

"If I were to say I had forgotten my glasses and had to rush back for them to my hotel which is only a block away, I could have a drink there."

"Oh, please, you can't," she said. The secretaries of very rich clubs are often sweet but slightly crushed by all the sables round the necks.

"Damn you," I said. "Can you run to two cups of strong black coffee in this very rich place?" And we giggled.

Ever since then I've done it on coffee. I enjoy myself less because I get less carried away and emotional, but my brain is ice clear and I am a better performer.

After you've made good on the platform the ladies of the committee are all over you. They've hired you from a brochure. Every season they get about 700 of these to choose from, and every brochure says the person is a genius and beautiful to boot. The committee is responsible to the club members. They're terrified you're going to be a flop because then, for one month, each time they go to the supermarket or the beauty shop they'll get attacked with dreadful reproaches. "We didn't think much of your choice last time, dear." And, "If that's the way you're going to spend our money. . . ." It seems the ladies go on and on about it.

After the lectures I get very chummy with the Madam Presidents and the secretaries. They're relieved I've been a success. They pour their hearts out. That's why I know so much about the lecture racket. In fact I know a lot too much about the lecture racket for the peace of mind of my agents.

American lecture agencies take 35 per cent of your fee, and you pay your own transportation and your own hotels and even the printing for your publicity. That is, the top agencies take 35 per cent: and you have to go to a top agency or else you don't get the big dates. Programme chairmen live in dread and horror of a lecturer having flu or breaking a leg. A top agency can send them a good replacement at the drop of a hat. Small agencies who only take 10 per cent aren't equipped for good replacements.

That 35 per cent sticks in my gizzard. Especially when it's snowing, and the road from the centre of Pittsburgh to the airport is one sheet of ice, and every inch is a hazard. And you've got to make that plane to get to the next date in time. I can see those agents up there in their New York offices, with the sun streaming in, sending out for boiling coffee. Pittsburgh is the saddest place in the world when it's snowing. But with all that steel they have a great many lecture clubs.

It must be admitted that lecture agents do have a difficult job. Some clubs have their meetings on the first Monday of the month, some every Wednesday and some on six Friday evenings during the year. So it's complicated to plan a tour during which the lecturer is kept busy continually for seven weeks, which is my yearly programme.

The first year you're with a lecture bureau it's a honeymoon. Big fees. Big dates. Little words of sweetness welcoming you in out-of-the-way places. "You got great notices in Port Huron. Well done."

You drool with gratitude and sign on the dotted line for next year. You say to yourself, "I did so well this year, what'll it be next year! Bigger and better fees. Good!"

Oh no! That's not the way it goes at all. If you're a success, your fees instead of getting bigger, tend to get smaller. You've become a bargaining lever. Not since the Roman market place has there been such dealing in human flesh. Between the different agencies the competition is cut-throat to capture the business of the innumerable ladies' clubs, universities, meetings, all clamouring for speakers. So it's "You want Ginette Spanier? She's expensive. But if you book so-and-so as well, or, better still, if you take all your speakers for the season from us, you can have them at a reduced price."

You've become part of a package deal. I know all this from the Madam Chairmen. It's the old commercial routine. I use the same technique at Balmain's: "You take one dress, it's so much. You take five: 10 per cent off."

But dresses are not made of blood and guts and nerves and the icy frozen road from Pittsburgh to the airport.

With Paul-Emile and Noël Coward at Le Bourget Airport

With Claudette Colbert and Donald Pleasance at The Plaza in
New York. That year I elected to wear a fringe which I now
realize was a mistake. My jacket was in white satin trimmed with
mink

At the Olympia Music Hall in Paris with Marlene Dietrich

So, why do I do it? Why, every year as the leaves turn brown, do I go wandering off alone all over the United States like a gypsy? First of all, there's the money. Then, it gets to be an addiction. When I see names like Spokane and Shreveport on my schedule, I can't resist.

It may be exhausting, but in a way it's a lazy life. You drop all your usual responsibilities. You're carted around like an expensive parcel. With time to think your thoughts. Then, there's the actual lecturing. To me, the actress *manquée*, the actual lecturing is intoxicating. It's not Sarah Bernhardt or Lynn Fontanne stuff, but don't let's underestimate it. It *is* part of the great world of entertainment. There's that minute just before you walk on, with them out there, hundreds of them, waiting for you—to destroy or applaud you. Sometimes it's students, teenagers, not the gentlest creatures in the world. Sometimes it's ladies. Sometimes it's mixed groups—men and women in evening dress. Those are the hardest. Men without their wives, or wives without their husbands are much easier. When they're together, and they're watching each other as well as you, then it's real hard work. But whoever they are, whatever they are, you must walk out there. There's no return. Get out there, girl, and get 'em.

And you stand there for over an hour juggling with your audience, every nerve taut, your brain click, click, clicking away, your concentration absolute. "Look relaxed, Ginette, even if the going's difficult." You get a laugh unexpectedly at a certain remark. An unexpected laugh, it's worth a million. So you put that remark in again next day. They don't laugh. Why? They should have. What did you do wrong? Breathed in the wrong place? Moved your hand an inch too much? Turned your head at the wrong moment? Then, there's that intoxicating moment when you get them. Now—keep them. If you succeed, they love you. When they love you, American audiences are so warm that they pump new life into you. So, you sign on the dotted line for next year.

F

That's the lecture business.

Also on the credit side of the whole larky lecture business is the opportunity it gives you to see and stay in places you'd otherwise never get to. Like Bozeman, for instance. Bozeman, Montana, is great. It is high up in the Rocky Mountains, and even the Lunts have never played Bozeman, Montana. One aeroplane a day goes in, and one goes out. No train. You change planes at a place called Billings. Many people have not heard of Billings, but I love airports like Billings. There's usually an enormous picture in crude colours of the first aeroplane landing there, with the horses terrified, rearing on their hind legs, and the cowboys crouching as the aeroplane approaches. You walk out to the gate nonchalantly, where quite a small plane, almost a private plane, is waiting for you. It's intimate and friendly. The little plane makes one stop before Bozeman, in a beautiful valley. You can't understand how it can land with the mountains and the trees crowding in, and suddenly it's on the ground, purring with pleasure, and perhaps two people get out. Just like a country station on an English railway.

It was icy cold the first time I landed in Bozeman. The airport is a hut in the middle of nothing. No porter, of course, but there was a delegation from the Montana State University to meet me: the French teacher. She was a French girl from Orleans who'd married a U.S. airman. She was mad about Bozeman. I kept thinking of Orleans on the beautiful River Loire and of Joan of Arc plucking the arrow from her breast as she won that city from the English. It seemed a long way from that expanse of ice and the Rocky Mountains. Also the best French pupil met me, and two young men from the university, and the lady who organized my lecture. She was a scientist. I was very touched.

My hotel in Bozeman was dark and old-fashioned, just like in a Western. Cowboys sat around in the hall reading newspapers, their legs stretched out in front of them, their cowboy hats either low down over their eyes, or angled at the back of their heads. Cowboys are very fancy with their high heels and the way they wear their hats.

As I walked in, the telephone was ringing. It was Claudette Colbert calling me from Palm Springs in the hot Californian desert, half America away!

The lady behind the desk gasped. She couldn't believe it was the real Claudette Colbert. Claudette had looked at the map and she said it was a straight line from Bozeman, Montana to Palm Springs. I looked at the map, too. I found the straight line, it seemed a very long one!

Claudette said that next morning I must hire a taxiplane to take me out of my particular corner of the Rockies, and at Salt Lake City I could take a plane to Palm Springs changing at Las Vegas. All those lovely names. It didn't seem possible, breakfast in the Rockies and lunch in the boiling sun. America is a very romantic country.

Bozeman, Montana has real ranches. I'd never thought of ranches except on the movies. Black Angus cattle are their speciality. Ever since Bozeman I am very attached to Black Angus. I spoke at the Montana University in the evening. After my lecture I was taken to a bar. It was very dark, with cowboys and their 'molls' sitting around and dozens of bottles of beer on the tables. I felt as if I was taking part in a movie. I couldn't believe it was 'real life'.

I asked my escorts if they could arrange the hiring of my taxiplane. I felt one hell of a girl hiring a personal taxiplane. Very early next morning I was driven out to the airport. It was even more deserted and icy than the day before, but beautiful, the sun glinting on the ice. And there before me, what did I see but Father Christmas in full dress, beard and all.

"What the devil are you doing here at eight o'clock in the morning in the middle of nowhere and in the month of November?" I asked.

"I'm trying to defreeze my helicopter," Father Christmas answered, gloomily. "The damn thing won't start and

I have to drop from the sky into the middle of a super-market 200 miles away."

America's not like Europe really.

Paul-Emile is not going to be pleased when he reads this bit, because taxiplanes is number one on his list of don'ts. Unfortunately his list of don'ts is not as short as it might be. Talking and laughing loud is number two. I often laugh quite loudly. Men are strange. They marry you just because you are adventuresome and a bit noisy, and then they try and change you. You can't change anybody. Result: one just takes taxiplanes and doesn't tell.

Paul-Emile doesn't believe that the real dangers of a lecturer's life are not the taxiplanes. It's being called for at the airport or at the hotel by the ladies. The sweeter they are, the worse they drive. They're in a bit of a flutter at meeting that dame from the Haute Couture in Paris. They expect me to be grand and rather stand-offish. So they borrow their husbands' cars which are models even newer-born than theirs. They're not familiar with them. Also they're fussed about their clothes with me coming from Paris, France. They're all dressed up with hats on and high-heeled shoes. Long manicured fingernails. Helpless hands because of modern gadgets like dishwashers and air conditioning.

The ladies always come in pairs to fetch me and the dialogue goes, "My! Irma, I just don't know where the starter is on Elmer's car."

And we go hurtling backwards or else violently forward. And when they find I'm not supercilious and grand we get very friendly and gossip like anything, and they miss the exit on the freeway, and before we know it we're twenty miles from where we should be.

But not all clubs give you a sweet welcome. I remember one club in West Virginia who greeted me with, "We're the toughest club this side of the Adirondacks."

I had no idea, nor cared where the Adirondacks were but was startled when they continued, "We pride ourselves on walking out after ten minutes if you can't hold our attention." And they ended, "We reduced Malcolm Muggeridge to tears."

This certainly makes one feel great as one is just going on to the platform.

Lecture clubs are often very geographical-minded, and mountains mean a lot to them. "We're the oldest club south of the Rockies" or "The biggest west of the Alleghenies". I never know if it's good or bad.

Another place which is exactly like the movies is Albuquerque, New Mexico. That's where most of the Westerns are made and where it all actually happened originally. It's still called the Santa Fé Trail, and you see the cleft in the mountains where the covered wagons went through with Red Indians attacking them from everywhere. The Indians are now in reservations with romantic Indian names, and people are taken to sightsee them. I hated it. They made me feel sad—and indiscreet. They had so much more right to be there than I had, and here was I looking at them and their sweet brown babies as if they were in a zoo. They were silent and impenetrable and tragic. The adobe huts were fascinating, built of red earth. Red earth everywhere. Red dust. And television aerials. The thought had never struck me that adobe huts would have television aerials. There were also turquoise jewels and the most brilliant Technicolor sunsets I have ever seen.

Santa Fé, the place, did not impress me one bit. Phoney. Artistic-phoney like St. Paul de Vence. Mexican-Indian artistic-phoney.

On the other hand I recall Cleveland, Ohio with affection. First of all I love those big tough towns and in Cleveland they gave me an autograph party. Usually I hate autograph parties. You sit there like a lemon, all dressed up, surrounded by piles of your own book, dozens of Ginettes grinning from the covers. You have to grin back at them. Pretty exhausting, keeping that grin glued on to your face.

I always feel that at autograph sessions they dress up the staff in hats and coats to play the crowd scenes. The same ones keep coming in and going out, like that poor horse in a cheap production of *Carmen*. He goes out stage left, is rushed madly round the back and comes in again panting stage right, trying to pretend he's a lot of horses.

In Cleveland they had my autograph session in the Crystal Room at the big department store over the railroad station. There I was sitting in the Crystal Room, all dressed up very fancy in a broché cocktail suit and spotless white kid gloves and a mink hat, with crystal chandeliers all over the place. My mink coat with the white lining was carelessly thrown over a chair. People came from quite far away. An old couple had driven for miles. They'd seen me on television they said, and they wanted to see what I looked like 'alive'.

It reminded me of the Brillat Savarin story: when the great chef went to the country for the first time he was asked what had struck him most and he said, "All those birds—raw."

The manager of the store was there and the undermanager and other staff buzzing around making a fuss of me when a lady came in and said, "Don't you recognize it?"

I was a bit amazed.

"It's a Balmain and it's too big," she shouted pointing at her dress.

The manager and the undermanager and the other staff were appalled. I wasn't there as a shopgirl, I was there as a star guest. I recognized the type of customer: very rich and swells in and out. Often when a lady is very irritable and shouts at you it's because she swells in and out. It's called 'going through a difficult time'. Noël Coward calls it 'our old friend menopause'.

Of course it can't be agreeable for the person to swell in and out, but for the couturier it's the bore of the world: letting out and taking in, and letting out and being shouted at.

In Cleveland in the Crystal Room I turned to the manager and the undermanager and the other staff and I said, "Bring me some pins. I'll do the fitting and your dress department can fix it."

The poor darlings were shattered, but they brought the pins. I ripped off my spotless kid gloves. I took off my mink hat—all very dramatic—I put the pins in my mouth and I knelt on the floor and did the fitting in front of everybody. It was difficult not to swallow the pins I was giggling inside so much. This was not at all what the swelly rich lady had bargained for. She had just wanted to attract rich-lady attention. After the fitting, not knowing how to get out of it, she rushed into the dress department and tried on some expensive dresses.

She came back to me with two and said, "Which of these should I have, Madame Spanier?"

I looked at her, and at the dresses, thought for a moment, and said, "They're both lovely but they have nothing in common. They're for completely different occasions. Why don't you have both?"

What could she do, poor lady, with everyone looking on? She had both.

The manager and the undermanager and the staff were delighted with me.

Early in my new career on the lecture platform Pan-Am made me a member of their Clipper Club. I was very proud. Some people have the Légion d'Honneur. Both are nice, but Clipper Club membership is more fun. The Légion d'Honneur does not provide you with hospitality in all the important airports of the world.

The nearest thing to the womb is the Clipper Club. It's always in the very heart of the airport building, far away from the outside world. Clipper Clubs are all decorated exactly alike, which is very comforting because you feel at home in whatever outlandish part of the world you find yourself: oriental-style grilling and indirect lighting behind a make-believe window. And air conditioning and

little paper napkins under the glasses and lots of ice inside
the glasses, and the hostesses marvellously welcoming.
After a few drinks you don't know whether you're in
Paris or New York.

Clipper Club members are very much the same all over
the world. Soft-voiced Americans. I've heard great conversations in Clipper Clubs.

"I asked for chocolate with my steak. He wouldn't give
it to me. So I gave him four good American dollars and
said I *want* chocolate with my steak."

"The number of black-faced sheep I've seen the last
weeks. And trout streams and grouse." A whole way of
life on the Scottish moors was revealed to me.

"If there's one thing that looks like a fjord, it's another
fjord."

"Greece is very nice."

I used to be shy on transatlantic flights. I've now
acquired technique. I put on slippers before I'm even out
of Paris, and I go to the toilet as soon as I'm allowed to
unfasten my seat belt. All the goodies in the toilet are
intact, wrapped in a cellophane bag. As Elizabeth Jane
Howard makes one of her characters say in her book *The
Sea Change*: "Goodness! Isn't it all beautiful? Neat
luxury." Pan-Am are angels to me. They give me VIP
treatment. Anyone can have VIP treatment in first-class,
but the height of VIP treatment is having it in Tourist,
being given that first seat in economy where you can
stretch your legs—and are only separated from the first-
class by a thin partition. In economy you hear better conversations than in first-class, but it must be admitted that
the wide seats of first-class are very comfortable. And
they have caviar.

Mind you, I don't like the way those hostesses in pale
blue close the folding screen between first-class and
economy each time they pass in and out. Ostentatiously.
"The sight of us isn't going to poison them up there," I
want to say.

But I love it when the hostesses give us instructions, that nasal voice over the inter-com proclaiming, "Every exit is marked with the word EXIT." Fancy. And, "Above the emergency exits are exact instructions as to how to open them—PULL." Very explicit!

Although most of the time I enjoy my travels and my travelling, one must not imagine that it is all beer and skittles. The overwhelming depression which comes over me when I open the cupboard in a strange hotel, and it's full of wire hangers from the cleaners, which collapse on to the floor as you try to hang up your coat. When it's wire hangers in the cupboard you know without going to look that it's not going to be all that clean and that the plumbing will be dreadful. Americans laugh at European plumbing, but there's a great deal of plumbing in America which the chic Americans don't know exists and which they could easily laugh at like a bad joke. And it's always in hotels where the hangers are wire.

So you're in one of these terrible hotels. And you can't relax because it's so beastly. And you think of your agents who have picked this hotel for you way back over there in New York City. And you think of them sleeping in their clean beds and taking 35 per cent. And love is not the feeling which fills your heart.

Take Oklahoma City. It was completely spoilt for me because of the filthy hotel. The kind of hotel where you don't trust anything, so you make up your eyes with soda water because you don't trust the tap water. Had I been in that lovely new motel skyscraper I saw from the car as I was leaving the city, I know Oklahoma City would have been my kind of town. Swinging. One bank has a gold roof. Another bank is made entirely of bulletproof glass, and you sit on a brown couch inside, press a button and get gently deposited in the vaults below, with all that money you've made out of oil tightly clasped in your hand.

Banks are a big thing in Oklahoma. It's no idle

statement in that town when a guy says to a girl, "You look like a million dollars."

The theme song of Oklahoma City should be Eartha Kitt's:

> But the music that excels
> Is the sound of oil wells
> As they slurp, slurp, slurp into the barrels.

It's the only city in the United States, in the whole world for that matter, where oil bubbles away under the Capitol building. The Capitol of Oklahoma City hasn't got a golden dome like all the other Capitols in the United States because, I was told, a Governor stole it. There it is, the Capitol, standing there domeless in the middle of Capitol Square, like any big building in the middle of any big square—the Opera in Paris for instance—and all around it, like enormous parking meters are . . . oil derricks pumping their hearts out. In the street. On the pavement. Dozens of them pump, pump, pumping away. They had a bit of trouble, it seems, with the derrick which pumps up the oil from under the Capitol building, because it had to be dug at an angle. I suppose they couldn't very well have the oil come spurting up out of the roof. It was very difficult to get me into that hall to lecture. I just wanted to stand there and watch those oil derricks pumping.

But although I am fascinated by the modern, vital business side of the U.S.A., there is an aspect of American psychology I distrust terribly—the good guy syndrome. For a start, to say it is unadult is putting it mildly.

You see two quite ordinary men meet by chance at an airport. What goings-on! They slap each other. They pummel each other.

"Well, Ed," one of them exclaims, "I'll be doggone! It's good to see you!"

"How've you been?"

"I've been fine. How've *you* been?"

"Great! I'm great."

"Ed, meet Phillip Jones."

"Hello, Phil."

"Hello, Ed."

"Nice meeting you."

"Good to know you."

I stand there amazed. Such joy. Such health. After a bit I long for someone to be called by an uncastrated name: Phil*ip*. Ed*ward*. And, maybe, just now and then, for someone to have a headache.

Why all this compulsive gaiety? This compulsive good health? What is it trying to hide? Fear, that's certain. It would seem that the American male does not have the courage to face up to real life, to the possibility of not being loved, to unhappiness, to the inescapable: sickness, old age, decay, death. Hence the Peter Pan complex. Hence the constant boys-together, good-guy, fraternal noises to shut out reality. When I was staying at the Dearborn Inn, Dearborn, Michigan, I saw men, important business men, meet for breakfast. The coffee room was crowded every morning with good guys who met there day after day for jocular breakfasts together. Terrifying.

One of the worst experiences of my life was finding myself one whole night in the middle of a Texan convention. I had arrived in the evening at a big hotel in Dallas, Texas, and I was shown up to my room. A little dream of a box. Perfect. The lighting, the TV, the radio, the bathroom, the writing paper, the tissues. All present and correct. But as I passed the open door of the room right opposite mine across the corridor I vaguely registered dozens of glasses and bottles laid out.

And then it began. Getting bigger and better and noisier and more ghastly as the night wore on. A convention. The Good Fellowship. The "Hi there's", "Come on in's" and "Hello there's" and "Yippee's". As the alcohol flowed, the noise increased. It was a nightmare of demented, drunken, screaming noise. And the cigar smoke, the cigarette smoke trickled under my door. I felt I was inside an enormous bell in hell.

I waited until midnight to ring the desk. Then I rang them every half-hour on the half-hour. I said, "Call the Police Department." "Call the Fire Department." "Call the Manager." Soft Texan voices 'ma'med' me the other end and obviously did absolutely nothing. Fool that I was, the hotel was selling the liquor.

Early next morning I went into the corridor and saw a Negro maid cleaning up the mess. Silently clearing away mountains of empty bottles left lying about by her masters—who don't think she is worthy to vote!

In the morning, when he deigned at last to arrive in his office, I called the manager.

He answered, "Al (then his surname, let's call him Brown) *Al* Brown speaking." So he, Alfred or Albert Brown, manager of a supposedly great hotel, was a good guy too.

"Mr. Brown," I said, "it has been my good fortune never so far to have had to spend the night in a bawdy house. I had to come to the your hotel in Dallas, Texas, for the experience." I said one or two other little things as well to Mr. Al Brown. As I rang off I felt he only just stopped himself in time from saying, "Thank you for staying at this hotel, ma'am."

Was I the only person to make a fuss, I wondered? Was I the only person to demand as my right a quiet night's sleep when I pay for a room in a hotel? Or, in America, is the party spirit so respected that revelry all night in the corridor of a hotel—not in a sound-proof room reserved for such junketing—is accepted and smiled upon as part of the national scene?

Another question I asked myself was: do you have to get together in a great big drunken huddle to sell motor tyres or an aeroplane part? Does an adult man with financial responsibilities really buy more because he's shouted yippee with a lot of fellow good guys? I find this difficult to

understand. And all those little folksy catch-phrases dis-
tilled like a gramophone record throughout the whole of
American life, do they really impress the people with their
sincerity? "Buy your second-hand car from Bert on Union
Street, the good guy." (Heard on the radio.) Does this
phrasing give confidence? Isn't a second-hand car dealer a
second-hand car dealer all the world over?

And what about the:

Thank you for flying American.

Thank you for flying Mohawk.

Thank you for travelling Greyhound.

Welcome to our Red White and Blue United Jet Liner.

Welcome to our Whisper Jet Golden Falcon Deluxe Day
Coach to New Orleans.

Have a good day now.

Have a good time now.

Have a good flight now.

Have a good trip now.

Once, I found myself answering, "So far it's been bloody
awful."

8

More American Notes

The other day, when I was in England, my family gave me a whole bundle of letters, notes and postcards I had sent them from America during various trips. Suddenly, completely forgotten impressions came rushing back at me.

A postcard with a ghastly view of Kansas City read: "I am waiting in the Greyhound bus station in Kansas City to get my bus to St. Joseph, Missouri. This makes a realist film look like *Alice in Wonderland*. All of America is *not* Fifth Avenue. Love. Ginette."

Oh, the depression of that grey Greyhound bus station. The dirt. The people shuffling about. But I remember my lecture in St. Joseph, Missouri. I had a standing ovation. My first. An unforgettable moment. So, it was worth it, that dingy bus station.

Another standing ovation I received was in Florida. That's a long story.

As I was leaving for my 1968 American lecture tour, I received my ticket and on it I saw Paris-New York-Melbourne. Obviously, I thought my stupid travel agents had made a ghastly mistake and were sending me to Australia, but, on looking a little closer I saw a tiny Fla after the Melbourne. Fla for Florida. Claudette Colbert was staying with us in Paris, and together we looked at the map of the United States spread out on the floor; but, not even with a magnifying glass, could we find Melbourne Fla.

Anyway, on the appointed day, I got to La Guardia Airport to take my appointed plane, and there I had to sit for six long miserable hours because there was snow in Atlanta, where in *Gone With The Wind* the sun never stopped shining. Those are things that happen to lecturers. Finally I did get to Melbourne, at three o'clock in the morning after a lot of free drinks because the airline wanted us to forgive them about the delay.

I felt quite lost arriving somewhere unknown in the middle of the night. But, there, waiting for me at the airport was a charming woman called Colette, who said she was French, married to an American, and she did not want somebody from Paris to arrive unmet. I told her that for nobody in the world would I get up to go to an airport at three o'clock in the morning. I was very touched.

We drove along a flat, causeway for miles and, suddenly, I saw a place lit up like the Château de Versailles. I was amazed. And, when we got nearer, what I took to be statues all lit up were . . . rockets!

Colette said didn't I know where I was? I said, "No; I hadn't been able to find Melbourne Fla. on the map."

Apparently I was at Cape Kennedy, and I was there to speak to the wives of Patrick Air Base. Patrick Air Base protects Cape Kennedy. Colette's husband was a helicopter hero. The first man to fly the Atlantic in a helicopter. The very day on which I arrived at Cape Kennedy it had been announced that the Americans were going to orbit the moon over Christmas. Generals from Washington and all over were on Cape Kennedy that day for the momentous decision, and the generals' wives were coming to hear me speak.

Now, I, Ginette Spanier, had been known to say often and very loud that flying to the moon as far as I was concerned was all right as a song title sung by Frank Sinatra but let them cure the common cold first before I'd start taking an interest in those gentlemen swimming about up there. And here I was suddenly at Cape Kennedy in a state of wild excitement.

When I spoke that afternoon I stood where astronauts had stood. And that's when I got the standing ovation.

I was supposed to leave for New York after my lecture, but the generals' wives said, "Stay. Dine with us tonight and tomorrow we'll have you shown Cape Kennedy like civilians don't often see it." Of course I did. One of the things I believe in most is *grabbing* at luck when it passes. If you don't you don't, deserve to have luck pass by and smile at you.

It was one of the most fascinating days I have ever spent. I, who knew nothing—but I mean nothing—was suddenly transported into another world, another age, another dimension.

The day before from La Guardia Airport I had written to my husband a whiny letter saying: "I'm too old for this sort of thing." Next day, I wrote him that I was over the moon with joy, and "over the moon" was the right expression.

I wonder what this means at the end of a letter: "P.S. Did you get 'the Shrine Mosque'? How's that for the name of a place in which to stand up and speak about Paris and the Haute Couture?"

Wherever could that have been? Where did I speak in a Shrine Mosque? It slowly came back to me. A place with a name like an illness. An illness which happens to teeth. Got

With Sammy Davis Jr. at Pierre Balmain's. There's always wild excitement when he comes to see me there (*Courtesy of Paris-Match*)

That first day in 1950 when Danny and Sylvia Kaye came to Pierre Balmain's. Pierre Balmain and I are at the back. Marie-Thérèse, one of our big stars, is on the runway

(*top*) A typical scene in the '*cabine*' at Pierre Balmain's. Small, squashed, overheated, hysterical but order seems always to come out of the chaos. (*bottom*) Showing an important customer to her place at the Collection. The seats under the mirror are the royal seats. Petra is on the runway (*Courtesy of Paris-Match*)

it . . . Peoria, Illinois. And I remember the brou-ha-ha about my coat.

It was an ordinary mink coat. Ordinary, that is, from the Paris Balmain point of view. It used to be dark, dark brown. Soft dark brown mink. But my hard-earned mink coat started to get slightly worn—from the Paris Balmain point of view, so I had it dyed black. It had buttons all the way down the front, because winter coats that flap open and let in the icy blasts are my idea of absolute nonsense. It also had two deep pockets because a winter coat into which you cannot slip essential things when it's raining—and you have to hold up an umbrella and everything is blowing and you have your hands full—is one great big nonsense. My sable coat has pockets too. The fact of a coat being made of mink seems to paralyse people's common sense. Cold is cold, winter is winter, whatever poor little animal is keeping you warm.

I used to wear my mink coat morning, noon and night, and round my knees in a train or car, and on my bed if there weren't enough covers. I wonder, now that I have a sable coat, whether I shall be quite so casual with it. I've had my mink coat made into a lining.

Now, this quite ordinary black mink coat, in a country called the United States of America, which is supposed to breed mink coats of unrivalled beauty, kind of stopped the traffic. Not on Fifth Avenue—but on aeroplanes and such-like. In Peoria, the girl at the desk of the Jefferson Hotel and Motor Inn whilst I was checking in said to me in a hushed voice as if she were in church, "Please, ma'am, what is that?" and she pointed reverently at my coat.

"Black mink," I answered. "So is my hat."

"Black mink," she shouted as if she were a cheer leader at a football game. "Black mink. It's black mink, folks."

So I said, "I'm coming down in half an hour to go and speak at the Shrine Mosque. Wear it till I come down."

That was a performance and no mistake. Before I went up, as she was peacocking around almost in tears, I said,

G

"My glasses are in the pocket. Could you let me have them please."

"In the *pocket*," she said. "It's got pockets?"

People keep on saying, "Mink is finished." "Mink is vulgar." "Mink is for football." Fools. Sex is one thing. Football is another.

There was another time when my mink coat put on a star performance. It was a year when Nancy Spain was with me. We had to change planes in Washington. Nancy had once said to me, "How is it that you understand America so much better than I do?"

"Because you only know New York and Hollywood," I answered. "Come trailing all round America with me on one of my tours, and you'll understand America too." And she came. It was lovely for me.

And here we were at the airport in Washington. But there was a mix-up with our tickets, and Nancy was a 'standby'. A 'standby' is the lowest form of animal life. You stand there in the hope of a seat being left free five minutes before take-off: and if there is, you are whisked on to the aeroplane in a breathless scurry.

Nancy and I stood there watching those capitalists with reserved seats walk unconcernedly by. Some actually laughed and chattered as they passed us on their easy way. One feels tempted to pray that one of them is going to fall down and break a leg!

I *had* to get on to that plane, because I was speaking in Jackson, Michigan next day, and I left Nancy standing there like a displaced person. Then, just before take-off, Nancy got on. There were wild whoops of joy, like meeting after years of separation. From the start it was a gay flight. One of those chic, commuter flights out of Washington. Almost all men. Men with sincere suits, mostly brown, very small lapels. Very small brims to their sincere hats.

"Wow, is that a coat," the air hostess said as she hung it up. And then the delicious announcement, "Would you like to pur*chase* (to rhyme with Chase National Bank) a cocktail?"

I have travelled more miles than can be counted backwards and forwards all over the United States, but I have never fathomed the why or the wherefore of, "Would you like a complimentary cocktail?" (free, and for nothing). "Would you like to pur*chase* a cocktail?" (one dollar). "Would you like to partake of a beverage?" (soft drinks—free).

This flight was the dollar deal. There was only one other woman passenger on the plane. A prim dame, unattuned to the atmosphere of the flight where most of the men—commuters—knew the hostesses. She 'purchased a cocktail' and gave the girl five dollars.

"Say, lady," the girl said, "you don't expect me to give you back change? I'll give it to you in drinks."

I almost hired her for Balmain's on the spot, but the lady was not amused. When the hostess brought us our drinks, she said:

"You're the one with the yummy coat, aren't you?"

"Wear it," I said. I remembered Peoria.

"You mean that?"

"Of course," I answered. And so she served us during the rest of the flight dressed in mink. Dinner came. Delicious. Everyone kept on purchasing cocktails.

When we were through, the hostess clapped her hands and said, "Come on, boys. Clear it away," and the gentlemen in their brown suits sprang to her command, whilst she leant up against the side, still in my mink coat, and, with an enormous wink at us, said, "I bet they don't do that at home."

I remembered, too, the little plane that took me from Peoria, Illinois, to Chicago. A bit shabby but cosy. They offered me hot chocolate and bouillon. I always drink hot chocolate on those little planes. Never anywhere else. Quite delicious. They also offer you chewing gum. William Little, one of the great men of the *Readers Digest,* took a charming interest in the project of this book of mine. He wanted me to call it *Chewing Gum and Hot Chocolate*. He loved my stories about America.

Usually I hate talking to anybody on an aeroplane. There was that time when I sat next to a most unattractive man with bad teeth. He kept trying to talk. But I'm not easily lured out of my silence when I'm travelling. I always write letters on a plane. It's quiet and peaceful. He kept looking and saw the envelope was addressed to France.

Up he chirped, "You represent a European concern?"

"Yes," I said.

"What do you do in Europe?" he said.

"I sell clothes." (It was easier to answer.)

He said, "I am a preacher so I represent the Lord Jesus Christ."

What does one answer to that? "Bully for you" or "Good luck!" Preachers shouldn't wander about with their collars turned the wrong way. I was glad when he got out at Buffalo.

Other letters bearing postmarks from all over the States jog my rag-bag of a memory.

. . . I had an audience of 10,000 at Provo University in Utah, last night. That's more than the Albert Hall will hold, I've found out. It was very moving, and absolutely terrifying. A student stood up and prayed for me before I started. Another student stood up and gave thanks for me when I finished. I wanted to cry. Nobody had ever stood up and prayed for me before. Afterwards they gave me a drink called a Shirley Temple or a Deanna Durbin, I don't remember which. I know it was a child star. It was made of cherry and ginger ale because they were Mormons. Mormons don't drink alcohol or coffee and there's something else they don't do, but I've forgotten what it is. I know there were three things. . . .

. . . In Seattle, Washington, they put my name up in lights over the Palomar Theatre where I was speaking. I turned the corner and suddenly I saw it. My heart missed a

beat. One of my dreams had come true. I mobilized everyone into taking a photograph of it and sent a print to Noël
Coward....

... Where you wait for the 'limousine' in Pittsburgh
Airport is like an underground lavatory....

... Heard on the radio after a few lines read from the
Bible: "The Bible can save you from directionless living—
Chevrolet"....

... In Kentucky the Negro bell boy said to me, "Ah
used to work around the race track and ah had a lot of
Italian friends. They taught me to drink Dago Red that
comes in those funny bottles"....

... I was at Bloomingdale's in New York buying a
nightie. In front of me at the counter a *distinguée* American
woman was talking in a soft slow *distinguée* voice. (In
America, *distinguée* ladies talk slowly and softly. In England
they talk rather high and loud. In France, they talk
affected.) The lady was saying, "I should like a nightgown.
A long one. Not one of those short ones, please."
The girl behind the counter snapped, "Plain or print?"
Her voice was neither soft nor slow.
The lady replied, "I think it should be plain because it's
for a nun."
The salesgirl snapped back, "They're wearing them print
now."...

... I wonder why it's romantic to be an air hostess and
lower than the gutter to be a house servant. A question of
altitude I suppose....

... You have to be strong-minded to travel all over the
United States when your name is Spanier Seidmann and
most of the hotels are called Sheraton and everything is
marked with an S. Those yellow bath mats with my initials
in the middle—beautiful. Don't steal, Ginette... don't steal.
Think of our mother, she brought you up so well....

... Funny thing about towels. The whole question of American towels is a mystery to me. I think about it quite a lot. In a country where comfort is a religion, why are the towels so small? There's nothing more luxurious, more voluptuous than a huge, all-enveloping towel. The Americans do, of course, make up in quantity for what they lack in quality. This makes for a pretty bathroom, with all those towels going from small to tiny spread around. Delicious colours. Pretty initials. But one thing I haven't acquired is the technique of drying myself in the United States: a towel round my neck, another round my middle, another drying my legs and all dropping off at the critical moment like a juggler with plates. The richer the house, the thicker the towels. When a towel is so thick and so embossed with gold and satin monograms, that it doesn't absorb water at all, then you know you're staying with a millionaire and you use Kleenex to dry yourself. ...

... Impressionist pictures are not really a status symbol any longer. There are so many of them around, they've become rather common. ...

... American men are pretty 'loungers'. They lounge against doorposts or in telephone booths. Many of them have very sweet little bottoms tightly wrapped in jeans. But, oh, how they telephone! Rows and rows of telephone booths everywhere, with men rushing in, putting their dimes in, pushing back their hats when they speak, rushing out again. Before the departure of their plane, they telephone. When their plane lands, they telephone. Is it Romeo business or dollar business I always wonder? ...

... In Spokane, Washington, I was taken dancing at the Elks. ...

... Between Rockford, Illinois and Chicago I was in a Greyhound bus bowling along the highway, cars rushing by. As far as the eye could see, an enormous, endless, treeless plain. A notice said: STRAY DEER. ...

. . . 1st December A Day in the Life of a Lecturer

New York　　Up at 6 a.m. Finished my packing mostly done the night before as usual (a principle).

7 a.m.　　Leave the house.

7.30 a.m.　　Pennsylvania Station. Ghastly. Three hours train journey to

10.20 a.m.　　Lancaster, Pennsylvania. Met by two ladies and rushed to press interview.

12 o'clock noon　　Luncheon with the committee who pepper me with questions for over an hour. This, before my lecture.

1 p.m.　　Asked to be excused before the very end of the meal. Lay on a couch in dressing-room. Slept for 15 minutes. Changed and made up.

1.30 p.m.　　Lecture. One and a quarter hours. Beat all attendance records.

2.45 p.m.　　Questions. Over an hour.

3.45 p.m.　　Driven thirty-eight miles to Harrisburg, Pennsylvania. Beautiful drive not on highway. Little roads.

5 p.m.　　Harrisburg Greyhound bus station. No comment.

5.30 p.m.　　Two hours drive through the night.

7.20 p.m.　　Arrive Chambersburg, Pennsylvania. Driven to Travel Lodge Motel. Delightful. Thirty minutes to change into evening dress whilst eating dreadful sandwich, and drinking dreadful cardboard cup of dreadful coffee. My sixth cup of coffee that day.

8 p.m.　　Welcomed by the Faculty at the Penn Hall College. Everyone in evening dress and tuxedos.

8.30 p.m.　　Lecture. Entirely organized by the students. Big auditorium. Full. Mostly teenagers. Some grown-ups. Introduced by President of College.

9.30 p.m.　　Questions. Many of them brilliant.

10 p.m.	Reception by the students crowded round me standing about or sitting on the floor. More and more questions. 'Shirley Temples' to drink.
11 p.m.	Party at President's house with some members of the Faculty. Charming. My first drink—the first of several.
1 a.m.	Bed after packing (principles are principles).
	19 hours. . . .

Yes, that Chambersburg Motel *was* charming, but I remember looking at my schedule one day and seeing that I was booked to stay at the Thunderbird Lodge, Medford, Oregon. Immediately I saw myself in a log cabin in the middle of rushing streams and redwoods, standing by the waterfall with the mission bell ringing, and a rambling rose in my hair like that lady in the song called "Ramona".

In fact it would be difficult for a rambling rose to grow anywhere near the Thunderbird Lodge, Medford, Oregon. The Thunderbird Lodge is situated at an intersection of two highways. There is a gas station outside and a restaurant called 'Sambo's'. The sign 'Sambo's' is enormous and twinkles in many colours night and day. The Americans are very extravagant with their electricity. In the night I heard a foghorn. "The sea," I thought. "Strange, I don't remember it on the map." I discovered it was the railroad passing right outside. American trains use their foghorns the whole time, even when it's quite sunny. I suppose American trains like to pretend they are ships. The Thunderbird Lodge, Medford, Oregon, is a big motel. There was a money box by my bed. I examined it carefully in case I could press button B and collect money someone else had put in. Pressing button B and someone else's money dropping out is almost as exciting as Las Vegas. But no. This is what it said on the money box: "Magic Fingers Massaging Assembly. It quickly carries you into the Land of Tingling Relaxation and Ease. . . .

Try it. You'll feel great. Twenty-five cents for a quarter of an hour." I tried it. It was ever so nice.

I lunched at 'Sambo's'. Gleaming clean and so pretty. Stainless steel. Coloured leather—well, perhaps not 100 per cent leather. Soft music. I by-passed Papa Jumbo's dollar special and settled for Sambo's special at seventy-five cents: six Sambo pancakes, one fresh ranch egg, two strips of lean bacon, Tiger butter and your choice of syrup. All on one plate. The waitress was dressed in spotless white like a hospital nurse and said, "Nice knowing you." She told me to put salt and pepper on the egg and pour Maple Syrup (that was the syrup of my choice) over the pancakes, all this on the same plate. Delicious. There were fleeting moments when the syrup had a slight flavour of pepper. "I can always diet in Paris," I thought. And all the time the hospital nurse poured me coffee. And the trains roared by hooting their foghorns, and the cars roared by and there wasn't only one gas station, I discovered: I counted five enormous gas stations: Standard, Texaco, America, Signal and Mobil. The Mobil sign never stopped turning around and around.

American bacon is one of my favourite things. At the bar a man sat eating a Jumbo Samboburger. He had on a wild shirt, a very butch belt and boots with highish heels. Oregon is in the Great North-west. One tends to forget it with all that hooting.

Behind me I heard a man's deep voice say, "As the Lord said to Noah when he said he couldn't row a boat, You never know what you can do till you try." As I got up to go, I looked to see what kind of child was the victim of all that wisdom. It was a little white-haired old lady. I couldn't help wondering what it was she hadn't tried to do.

A 'kind of interesting' remark, I thought. "Kind of interesting" is a vastly overworked description in the States. They use it to describe all manner of things. Abstract pictures. Jewels, furniture. And the zipper on the left side of my dress. In the Haute Couture we like to hide our zippers in a seam instead of that gash down the middle of the back. "The way your zipper goes is kind of interesting," they exclaim. And I turn round and they zip it down and they zip it up, fascinated at how interesting it is. In St. Paul's, Minnesota, in a blizzard, some of my audience followed me in the street and made me take off my coat then and there, with the snow falling like a thick white curtain. Just so they could see my zipper on the left half-back instead of centre full-back.

To me, St. Paul's is one of the most romantic cities in the United States. It is the home of Scotch Tape and the Mississippi River. Can you ask for more than that? You see an ordinary river, sort of grey. Out of politeness, you ask its name and, behold, it's the Mississippi. You see an ordinary factory, sort of grey, and, out of politeness, you ask what it makes, and it's Scotch Tape. Too much for one town. When I was lecturing in St. Paul's—to an audience of 9,000 which is a lot of people sitting there all together—after they'd played the *Star Spangled Banner*, a tall, thin, good-looking man, clean American type, wearing an alpaca suit in the middle of winter, came up on to the stage carrying a huge, gift-wrapped box. The cameras clicked and he said he was a director of the Minnesota Mining Company, the makers of Scotch Tape, and they'd heard I loved Scotch Tape and they were honoured to present me with a selection of their products. A kind of highlight it was.

I get quite a lot of presents during my travels. In Kohler, Wisconsin, where the bath fittings come from, they gave me an ashtray in the form of a bath tub. It weighed a ton, and had I brought it back all the way to Paris, with the overweight, it would have cost me as much as made in pure gold. As I went round the Kohler factory I hinted shamelessly about being given a tap—a 'faucet' as they call it in America. American faucets 'send' me in no uncertain way. But no, I was given a bathtub ashtray instead. In Akron, Ohio, I was given an ashtray in the shape of a motor tyre. (Akron is where motor tyres are made.) And I don't smoke. Binkie Beaumont says that if I had real sex appeal I wouldn't get all those ashtrays. Some ladies, he says, get diamonds.

In this hotch-potch of correspondence I found a letter from Chicago and another from Fall River, Massachusetts. People are very cross when I say I am in love with Chicago.

But, the first time I went there I *did* fall in love with Chicago. Those tall buildings right on the shore of the lake which might be the sea . . . it's so vast. Some mornings misty gold with sunshine, deep snow the next, and me on every programme, television and radio. Chicago in those days had two main airfields, and you went from one to the other by helicopter. I adored that. I spoke at the Ladies Athletic Club and expected football boots with spikes to be lying around. I couldn't have been more wrong. The Ladies Athletic Club in Chicago is the acme of sables-round-the-neck. One of the ladies invited me to drinks in her penthouse way up above the lake and the factories, and even above the Wrigley building. "My little house in the sky," she called it. She had one of those names which conjure up American railroads and marble palaces on Fifth Avenue.

There was an oil-painting of a lady hanging on the wall. I know absolutely nothing about paintings. The lady in the picture wore a sweeping skirt and a high collar, one felt the corsets underneath. I thought I couldn't go far wrong if I said in a cultured sort of way, "A Sargent, I presume."

"No, *that's* not the Sargent," my hostess said. "That is the Sargent over there."

"Beautiful," I murmured. I meant it. It was a great portrait.

"I cut off the legs to fit that wall," my hostess added. I imagined a sale at Sotheby's: "Legs by Sargent."

I am not in love with Chicago any more, because I was in Chicago when I heard of President Kennedy's assassination. The place where you heard of President Kennedy's assassination is like a wound. It will never heal, that moment when the truth sank in.

When I was going to speak in Fall River, Massachussetts, I was told by my friends not on any account to mention Lizzie Borden. Lizzie Borden was that girl who was supposed to have killed her mother and father with an axe. It could never be proved: so, if Lizzie did it, she got away with it. Agnes de Mille wrote a ballet about it called *Fall River Legend*. I don't remember a lot about that ballet except that in her mind Lizzie kept on seeing her mum and dad dressed as bride and bridegroom, and it upset her dreadfully. The axe was enormous. She kept dragging it around the stage. It was a psychological ballet.

Fall River is not far from Boston. I was staying at the Ritz in Boston because Lena Horne and Lenny Hayton were there. I went to their show three times in two days. To me Lena is just about as beautiful as you can get, and Number One entertainer as well. Lovely, complicated, difficult Lena. When her autobiography appeared and I found that "Ginette S." was among her dedications, it gave me such joy. The Ritz Hotel in Boston is famous because it is the only one in the U.S.A. where you ring the bell for maid, valet or waiter, instead of telephoning room service. This is very European and civilized. In Boston the clam chowder is delicious, and they sell live lobsters at the airport instead of perfume and liquor as at other airports. They pop them into a special cardboard box, like a wig box, except that it has holes so that the lobsters can breathe.

People are always telling you that Boston is exactly like England. . . .

Anyway, one of the ladies from the luncheon club came and fetched me at the Ritz in Boston and drove me to Fall River. It was a lovely day. Autumn in America is more beautiful than one can imagine. I kept on reminding myself to shut up about Lizzie Borden.

When we approached Fall River the lady said to me, "I suppose you would like to see the house where Lizzie Borden was born?" She told me a lot of interesting facts about Lizzie Borden, such as that at the autopsy they found Mr. Borden had eaten eel stew for breakfast.

"They knew it was for breakfast," she said, "because he never got to having his lunch."

Also that poor Lizzie had to move after the incident because little boys kept throwing stones at her window.

"Where did she move to?" I asked.

"Two blocks away," she answered.

The committee gave me lunch before my lecture. A lady in a shaped brown mink stole told me that Lizzie Borden was really a saint: she'd left all her money to preserve animals. "And no wonder," she added, "after the humans had been so cruel to her."

Opposite her, another lady in a shaped mink stole, only grey, got quite red in the face. "She was a monster. She murdered her mother and father, and it's because of her damn money that we're infested with squirrels."

She was a saint. She was a monster. I suppose those two ladies meet every day in the High Street, and they've never been able to agree about Lizzie Borden.

Once Josh and Nedda Logan gave a buffet lunch for me in their apartment high above the East River. It was, of course, the Logans who started it all, my second life. They came and had drinks with us in Paris back in 1946 or 47 and told me to write our war experiences. It became *It Isn't All Mink*, and it started me on my hammy life; so here I was lunching with the Logans in New York, saying, "Now I must go and get to the airport."

The Logans don't really believe in my lecture life, but they laugh indulgently at me.

Quite a few people can't understand what it's all about.

Larry Olivier once said to Noël Coward: "How's all this going to end with Ginette?"

And Noël answered,

"A nervous breakdown, my dear, a nervous break-down."

It's obvious that they haven't sold dresses to ladies from ten in the morning till seven at night every day for years. That *is* a strain.

"Where are you off to now?" Nedda asked

and I said, "To a place called Sewickly."

And everybody exclaimed,

"There can't be a place called Sewickly."

A lady who was there upped and said, "There certainly is, and, what is more, we have a house there." It was Mrs. Heinz of the fifty-seven varieties.

"Cancel your reservation, Madame Spanier," she continued, "because my husband is going there this very evening in his private plane, and he can give you a lift."

Getting a lift in a private plane is just about the most luxurious adventure a lecturer can have. Mr. Heinz and I drove to La Guardia Airfield, but not the usual La Guardia —a private bit. Like having a private beach at Antibes. A beautiful man in a pale-blue uniform, who was waiting for us, took my bags out of the taxi (I have very chic luggage so I didn't let down the side). I discovered it was the captain. It gave me quite a turn having my bags carried by the pilot.

In no time at all we were off. I lay on a sort of chaise-longue with my feet up sipping Scotch and soda. No pain, any of it. And I learnt a great deal about millionaires. To them the two dirtiest words in the language are 'flying commercial'. A low plebeian habit.

I see a great deal of the Joshua Logans when I am in New York. One year they gave a big party for Princess Margaret and Lord Snowdon. I went to it. So did the whole of show business and that included Tommy Steele and Sammy Davis Junior. I wore a long scarlet wool evening dress. Shortly after Merv Griffin invited me on to his television show to be interviewed about the party, and he asked me to wear the long scarlet wool dress. Merv Griffin has one of the most important television shows in the United States—a night show with guests—and is extraordinarily attractive into the bargain. He generates such enthusiam and loyalty amongst the team of people who work for him that the whole thing is a party. There were eminent people on the show that night: Louis Untermeyer the poet, witty and brilliant at 80; Melvin Belli, the flamboyant attorney who defended Jack Ruby.

A big television show is a nerve-racking experience.

I went to make-up and then waited for my turn, looking in on the programme on a monitor set in a small waiting-room, unable to sit down for fear of creasing my dress. I felt like a father waiting for his wife to have a baby upstairs. Except that I was waiting to have my own baby. My turn came. The star spot. I don't deserve such exalted treatment, but Merv Griffin spoils me. Merv started to introduce me—"The most sparkling French woman . . ." —and I walked on. I caught my heel in the nylon curtain, and the whole thing nearly crashed down around me. Merv Griffin roared with laughter. I died inside. And Merv Griffin started his introduction over again: "The most sparkling French woman, in fact, one of the most sparkling women anywhere I have ever met is Ginette Spanier . . .". This time a real crash. The couch on which Louis Untermeyer and Melvin Belli were sitting collapsed completely, landing them on the floor. Pandemonium. The whole theatre in stitches, Merv Griffin overjoyed. Me completely shattered. Standing there like a fool all the limelight taken violently from my sparkling person. The cameras zoomed enthusiastically away from me and focused on the great Mr. Untermeyer sitting on the floor. I kept standing there, an idiotic grin glued on to my face, death and murder in my heart. That, it seems, was real big, live television stuff.

And Merv Griffin introduced me a third time. "The most sparkling French woman . . .".

The next time I was on the Merv Griffin Show was with Cassius Clay. No one crashed anything and it all went swimmingly. Cassius Clay is very beautiful.

In all the years I've been lecturing, with all the tight schedules, and cancelled planes and trains breaking down, only once have I been late on the platform.

I was to speak at Battle Creek, Michigan. That's where the Corn Flakes come from. Like the conscientious lecturer I pride myself to be, I left New York the afternoon before my lecture. It's a terrible temptation to cut things fine and stay an extra night in New York, but principles are principles. So, on a fine Sunday afternoon I found myself on Kennedy airfield sitting in a jet bound for Detroit, my safety belt fastened and my dollar bill slipped into that little envelope, with an 'x' opposite 'Scotch and soda'. Suddenly, dramatically, before we'd had time to take off, a thick black fog descended obliterating the earth, the sky, the sun and the aeroplane in front of us on the runway. America is a violent continent. After about an hour of sitting there like unhappy toothpaste inside a tube, the aeroplane crawled back to the gate—and very frightening it was too, with all those monsters we knew to be moving about all round us, invisible in a sudden ghostly world. In the space of a few minutes New York had been blacked out, the three major airfields closed. The airport when we finally got back to it was like an anthill into which a giant had given a careless kick: me not the calmest amongst those hundreds, those thousands of stranded travellers scuttling about hysterically. I fought tooth and nail to get a booking on the first aeroplane out next morning, provided aeroplanes left next morning. No mean feat, but I'm a pretty determined woman.

So, at dawn, a foggy dawn, I went through the old departure routine again, having during the night received frantic telephone calls from my lecture date. They had arranged to have a private aeroplane waiting for me on Detroit airfield ready to whisk me off to Battle Creek—

On the Pont Alexandre III in Paris
Photograph by Richard Avedon

My name in lights outside a theatre at last!

Jenny winning at Newmarket

provided I managed to get on to that first plane. I did. The fog had lifted in the nick of time.

Feeling like a secret agent, I swapped planes at Detroit airfield, and we flew off to Battle Creek low over a sunny Michigan State. We were in constant touch with the theatre where I was to speak, our progress being reported to the assembled audience: "They're over so-and-so." "They'll be arriving in a quarter of an hour, in ten minutes, in five minutes . . .". We landed. From plane to car to theatre I was hustled. And I 'was on'—twenty minutes late. There's never been such an entrance.

After the show, at a party given for me, there was caviar. I always remember the places where I have caviar.

New Orleans. It's all true—the beauty, the magic, the charm of New Orleans. The Vieux Carré, the French Quarter. The wide, wide Mississippi River, not grey like at St. Paul, Minnesota. The balmy air and the proud Negro boys, strolling on Bourbon Street. The lace-like *fer forgé*, the balconies, the slender columns, some round, some square, some black against the red brick houses. And southern hospitality. That's true too. A customer at Balmain's had said to me, just like that, "If ever you come South, spend a weekend with me in New Orleans." I did.

From the moment the loudspeaker in the aeroplane said, "Will Madame Spanier on landing please contact the ground hostess" to the moment four days later when that same hostess saw me on to another plane, I had what is called 'a ball'. When I left I felt I was leaving dear, sweet, long-lost friends. They make such a fuss of you. An hour after I arrived there was a private dinner party with delicious food in a penthouse overlooking the whole of New Orleans and the Mississippi River. My host had sent his maid whilst I was unpacking to iron my dress. Then all the famous names: lunch at Galatoires; coffee at the French Market; Sunday brunch at Brennans; a dinner for me at Antoine's. Drinks in one private room. Dinner in another.

H

With all the great Louisiana dishes, culminating in a
Baked Alaska with '*Bienvenue*' written on one side and
'Ginette' on the other. And this from someone who had
only met me at Balmain's. I sat next to the celebrated Doctor Ochsner. The Ochsner Foundation is one of the great
hospitals in America. Sweet he was, in his red velvet dinner
jacket. "Have you any relatives called Spanier in the United
States?" he asked me.

"No", I answered. "Outside of my mother and my
sister I haven't any relations in Europe either." He looked
pensive. And he started again:

"I had a patient called Spanier. It's the only time I've
heard that name. He was kind enough to say I had saved
his life."

"Fancy," I answered. I was rather irritated. I have
absolutely no '*esprit de famille*'.

He went on, "Are you sure you don't know anyone
called Spanier? My patient is very well known. He's a
musician. Calls himself Muggsy Spanier."

"Put on your glasses," I shouted. "Look at my bracelet."
A gold bracelet which never leaves me, with Muggsy
engraved on it. Given to me by Lena Horne. All the jazz
people—Louis Armstrong, Lenny Hayton, Lena—call me
Muggsy after the famous trumpeter Muggsy Spanier.
Ochsner and I, delighted, were talking at the same time.
"I've never met him," I said. "Everyone sends me his
records, his photograph. Where is he?"

"In Sausalito, California. Let's phone him." Three
minutes later, from New Orleans, Louisiana to Sausolito,
California (look at the map, that's America and the Bell
Telephone Company for you).

"Muggsy? This is Doctor Ochsner. Here's Muggsy to
speak to you."

"My twin, my twin," I exclaimed.

And he said, "I saw in the papers you were speaking in
San Francisco last week, but by the time I found out where
you were, you'd gone. All my friends talk about you."

The following year Muggsy Spanier died. I am so glad that at least I had that telephone conversation with him.

Then in New Orleans there was Bourbon Street at night. Me on Bourbon Street. The air was soft and warm. I went to Preservation Hall. I went to Dixieland Hall. I saw the Old Men. I heard the Old Men. Play jazz. My kind of jazz. I wanted to cry. It was so beautiful. It didn't seem like a tourist trap like Pigalle. It was friendly and gay, and there was music. Papa Celestin is dead. Louis Armstrong has left, but Barbarin and all the other old men are still playing their hearts out. Dixieland. The real stuff. You skip the cheap strip joints. You walk in where the music comes from. Sometimes it's a kind of drill hall with benches. You pay a dollar. You sit on a bench or on the floor. You stay as long as you like. Sometimes it's seats all around an enormous horseshoe bar with the musicians on a platform in the middle. I couldn't be dragged away.

Thinking back on my lecture tours I can't help wondering why there is all this ironical laughter each time I mention them.

"You and your ladies with flowery hats! They'll listen to anything."

A French girl-friend, when someone asked whether I made the same speech everywhere, answered, "Have you seen the map of America? Ginette can go on boring those American women for years with the same old speech."

Madame, I speak ad lib, so no two lectures are ever exactly the same. At each place I have to feel my way with my audience and adapt the things I say to their particular climate. And ladies' clubs are only a fraction of my activity. We of the lecture platform speak to schools, colleges, universities, also to what is called mixed groups. So hush your silly laughter. Look at your own hat . . . what's that for a little *numéro*?

And, as we're talking of the ladies, what strikes me each time I walk on to a platform, apart from gratitude at so many people coming to hear me, is . . . where else would you find large numbers of women taking such an interest in subjects ranging from politics to antique silver, passing through literature and Haute Couture? Nothing would induce *me* to leave my home in the morning to listen to some strange woman talk about herself—or anything else. Yet there they sit, hundreds of them, neat and tidy, even all dressed up when it's to hear someone like me who, they think, sets great store by elegance. They've hurried through their chores, got their children off to school, left a meal prepared if one of the family comes home to lunch. Their houses are spotless. I know this for a fact because time and again in the most varied corners of the United States I've gone to their homes unexpectedly. You'll argue that most of the stuff dealt out on the lecture platform is not of a highly intellectual nature. Granted. But is everything you look at on television highbrow? You'll argue that all that stuff they listen to does not sink in very deep. Granted. But to sit there quietly and ask intelligent questions is, after all, as good a way of passing the time of day as gossiping with your neighbour over the garden fence, or spending hours on the telephone talking to your girl-friends.

And I am going to wave another flag in favour of my American ladies. I know their reputation for being bossy and matriarchal, for emasculating their menfolk, that's none of my business, it's between them and their menfolk. But we must recognize one thing—the tangible results brought about by their energy. American hospitals, American universities. City orchestras. Who collects the money? Who works ceaselessly to bring these about? Let's face it— the women. Just stop a minute before you write off my women listeners with an amused shrug of your sophisticated shoulders.

9

My Friends, My Faults

This new existence of mine: travelling, lecturing, radio, TV appearances all over England and America, is, of course, only secondary to my real life: my life in Paris, my home and my work at Balmain. Much as I love it all, it is pretty exhausting.

One Saturday morning in the spring of 1964 Paul-Emile and I were so tired that we decided to go to the coast for thirty-six hours. We both needed a good blow of sea air and a quiet night's sleep, so we headed towards Trouville without even leaving our telephone number in Paris.

After a lunch of warm shrimps and fish and cool white Muscadet wine, I went up to my room to sleep, and Paul-Emile went off for a walk. He had hardly gone when the bellboy ran after him in the street and brought him back to the hotel. He came up to the room: Marlene Dietrich wanted him personally on the telephone. As he took the call his face went terribly grave. I realized something dreadful had happened.

"She'll call you back," he said, and replaced the receiver gently on its cradle.

Nancy Spain had been killed that morning, the day of the Grand National, in a small private aeroplane which had crashed on Aintree Racecourse as it was landing. 21st March 1964. Not being able to get me on the telephone, the *News of the World* had rung Marlene and had asked her to find me and give me the terrible news. Marlene knew we had gone to Trouville. She had taken the telephone book and rung every hotel in alphabetical order until she found us.

For many of us, life will never be quite the same without Nancy Spain.

The BBC asked me to do Nancy's tribute for "Woman's Hour" on a direct line from Paris. The head of BBC Paris at the time was Noble Wilson, and I shall never forget his kindness to me.

When London came through on the microphone he said, "I've got Ginette Spanier here. Just wait a minute." Then he handed me a swig of neat whisky, said "Drink it up", and held my hand tight during the whole of my broadcast.

I lost so much with Nancy's death, but I could not let it lose me England too. Nancy and England were intertwined for me. I was scared of going back there with Nancy gone. This, however, was one of the things which had to be faced. The contracts were signed, and up to the North I went two weeks after that dreadful Grand National Day. It was too soon.

Everywhere I went I was shown Nancy's signature in autograph books. Messages were given to me, "When Ginette Spanier comes here, give her my love."

I found I couldn't bear to be alone, even in my friendly Lancashire triangle. So I would commute back to London by the late Manchester plane. Lena Horne was appearing at the Palladium. I'd get to the Dorchester around one o'clock in the morning when Lena and Lenny Hayton, her husband and musical director, were just back from the second show. We'd sit in our dressing-gowns talking over a quiet night-cap. They had an extra room in their suite— not a room, just a little box with a bed and a telephone— where they put me up. The next day before they were awake I'd go up North again.

The most unexpected people were kind to me. Take David Jacobs, the radio and television personality. I'd known him some time, but we'd hardly met outside a studio. He knew Nancy Spain well. After her death, he felt I must be depressed, and he just turned up. Extraordinary.

David Jacobs was one of the first to interview me on television when *It Isn't All Mink* came out. It was on Lorna Pegram's "Wednesday Magazine". (I remember I was on the programme with Marghanita Laski, and we did not agree about a thing.) Once, the whole team of "Wednesday Magazine" came over to Paris, and we did the programme from the roof of one of the big stores overlooking the Seine. Meant to be "Paris in the Spring" —all light dresses and printed organza—we hit on one of those icy days and froze to death on our rooftop, wrapped in furs and woollies.

I continue to lecture a great deal in England. I once had my horoscope read and was told, "Your travels are your medicine." This is specially true of my trips throughout England.

Nancy Spain had said to me, "You're always saying you're so homesick for England. What do you know of England? London and Sussex. That's not England. Go north and see what England is really like."

So I went North. She was right. Not that I don't love

the South, but the South is easier. The Midlands, the North are made of tougher stuff. And when they love you up there, they certainly let you feel it.

I suppose the chairwomen of the different clubs get together and exchange views on speakers, because, in Lancashire, one of them said to me, "We knew you'd be good because Mrs. So-and-So from X told us that three of their members, who always fall asleep during lectures, kept awake right through yours." I should like to thank those three unknown Lancastrian ladies who, by *not* nodding off, spread my fame throughout their countryside.

Each time, as I crisscross England, it is a serious emotional experience. Sitting alone in my train, I am absurdly vulnerable, stripped of the inner protection afforded by my usual activity. The different accents of England. The green dampness of the countryside in spring. In winter, the browny, soft, *taupé* colours (*taupé* is that furry felt of which old-fashioned hats were made). The horror of the black country between Manchester and Sheffield where, at those broken down coal stations, the workmen come on to the train laughing and joking. The imagination of the wild get-ups of the young. (These now over-advertised clothes reached London long after I had seen them in the North. Paris and New York woke up to them two years later still.) Sometimes, opposite me in the train, a beautiful adolescent: trousers, longish haircut. Boy? Girl? Strangely attractive, mysterious. Some of the girls at those miserable stations have lovely, long, shiny hair.

The interminable waits for connecting trains. The depressing, draughty platforms. The almost forgotten taste of boiling Bovril in a crowded buffet. The woman behind the counter saying:

"There you are, luv."

As I travel alone around England, my thoughts, those little gleaming fish in my fishpond of a mind, dart around unrestrained.

As I sit alone in trains I think about my friends. Noël

Coward constantly comes to the surface. He is one of my great loves. My friendship with him is one of the joys of my life. Every time we've been together has, for me, been unalloyed enjoyment—with the exception of one hour when he took me out to dinner and wagged his finger at me. I suppose I had it coming to me: I had seen him do it to so many of the people he loved and he used to say, "Don't look so smug. Your turn will come. It's just that, so far, every time I've wanted to tell you what I thought of you, somebody next to you did something terrible and got priority." So my turn came. It wasn't pleasant, but at least I didn't cry. I was very near to it.

Otherwise it's been glorious, even on occasions when with anyone else it would have been awful. Like on that terrible journey from London to Paris on a boiling hot Sunday in July—Noël, Margaret Leighton and me. London Airport a *Kafkaesque* horror—dirty, noisy, crowded, beastly, holiday trippers shoved around in hordes, and our plane delayed for hours.

Maggie kept on saying, "It's like *The Consul.*" (Menotti's opera).

Of the three of us, Noël was the only one to stay unruffled, even though terrible bores, seeing him trapped, pinned him down with a ruthless lack of discretion. Because of Noël we laughed the whole time.

So many souvenirs, like once getting into the Savoy from Paris and finding a message in my room, "Dinner in Mr. Coward's suite at 8.45." I unpacked, bathed and changed, with my heart singing. Young enough still to get excited, old enough to enjoy it all without worrying about inessentials. When one is young, how much enjoyment is ruined by unimportant details being blown up tragically into exaggerated proportions!

Noël awaited me, dressed fittingly in an exotic dressing-gown, saying, "Let's have oysters." And the table was rolled in like in so many Coward scenes. If only the me of 1924, I thought, could have seen this, or could have known that Noël Coward would lend me his flat whenever I went to New York.

So many lovely Coward occasions, in London, Paris, New York, Wisconsin, Switzerland, Philadelphia, Jamaica. Hours of brilliant Coward talk, of Coward wit, of Coward music, of Coward listening to and laughing at my stories. And always, underlying it all, Noël's wisdom and affection and understanding.

Places are divided into two for me: places I go to, and hate, and want to be out of immediately, or places I go to, where I feel happy, and sit back and purr.

Into this latter category comes the Lunt home in Wisconsin. How can I describe Alfred Lunt and Lynn Fontanne to those of this generation who may never have seen them act? They are the aristocrats of the theatre. They are the greatest acting couple in the world, unequalled, unparalleled.

They live in Wisconsin, U.S.A. and have imbued every corner of their home with their magic. It is beautiful and comfortable and welcoming, and my heart is warmed wherever I look and saddened when I have to leave. Not that I can describe any of it, I am so enchanted by Alfred and Lynn that I haven't attention left over to notice the inanimate objects' around.

A weekend I spent with them stands out. Noël Coward was there, and I was allowed to share the intimacy, if only for two days, of those three greatest among the great *monstres sacrés* of my time. I arrived on a winter's evening. We sat in the library, a fire burning in the fireplace. There was an oil-painting of Lynn by Jane de Glehn over the mantelpiece. (De Glehn had painted *me* when I was young.)

"That was you in *Dulcy*, wasn't it, Lynnie?" Noël asked.

"Yes, of course," she said. "My first success, remember?"

Then Noël went on to recall how they were all three in New York in 1921. Penniless. And Lynn Fontanne got the lead in a play called *Dulcy*. All their hopes were pinned on her being a success in the play. On the first night, Alfred and Noël sat in the last row, holding their breath. They need not have worried, *Dulcy* was a smash, and Lynn Fontanne became a star overnight. Shortly afterwards, in Lynn's dressing-room, they were discussing a new detail Lynnie wanted to put into the second act, and Noël, loathing having to do it, interrupted her and asked her to lend him twenty dollars. He was flat broke. Lynn fished into her handbag, gave Noël the money and went straight on with the conversation. The very next day Noël sold his first short story and immediately went to the theatre to repay Lynn.

"What's that for?" she asked. She had been so engrossed working out the bit of comedy she was planning that she never even noticed dipping into her bag for Noël's twenty dollars.

I sat there entranced as those three laughed and talked and reminisced. I was living these moments with the original cast of *Design for Living*, I who love star quality.

I remember the first time I went to the Lunt home. I had been speaking in Kohler, Wisconsin. That's where the bath fittings are manufactured, as you will remember. The great Mr. Kohler himself, when he heard that I knew the Lunts, was full of respect for me and lent me a car to go and visit "Wisconsin's two most prominent citizens". Alfred had told me over the telephone to ask where the house was at the general store by the crossroads. So the chauffeur got out and asked could they tell him how to get to the home of Mr. and Mrs. Alfred Lunt.

"I can, but I won't," said the storekeeper.

"Why?" said the chauffeur.

"We don't want them bothered," was the answer.

It was only after having been assured that I was expected, that I was spending the night at the house, and after the man had come out and looked me over slowly through the window of the car, that we were given the directions and allowed to drive on.

Another of my English friends whom I miss sadly in Paris is Hugh Beaumont. I have known him half my life, and I take an immense pride in his career. Binkie Beaumont is one of the most powerful theatrical producers in England. He is good-looking, perfectly groomed and interested in everything. As he is one of the only people to be an intimate of both my sister Didine and myself, he gets two opposite views on the subject of our childhood. It fascinates him.

All those years of fun together. All those years of theatrical excitement, of peaceful days in the country at his house in Essex. Binkie is the only one who worries about my financial situation. Nobody ever worries about me: people either think I'm rich, or else it's "Ginette's all right. She'll get by!" But Binkie worries, and as soon as he's had a couple of drinks, he gets me on the carpet and begs me to be less extravagant. I remember one boiling hot day at Binkie's country house when everyone else played tennis in swim suits it was so hot, whilst Binkie and I sat and gossiped.

Keith Baxter was skipping about on the tennis court, and I kept exclaiming, "One day Keith will be a great star. Mark my words. He's so beautiful in his sinister Welsh way."

And Binkie said, "Now, don't be silly, Ginette. Concentrate. Promise me you're going to start saving some money."

Then we all piled into an open car to go and bathe in a neighbouring municipal swimming pool. That was before Binkie had his own pool.

As we rushed through the summer country lanes, Keith Baxter exclaimed, "When one was a child, this is what one imagined grown-ups lived like *all the time*!" I loved that remark, and I reminded Keith of it when, in 1966, I saw the Orson Welles film *Chimes at Midnight* with Keith playing Prince Hal brilliantly: that mixture of youth and tenderness and inherent royalty.

Keith wrote to me after the film: "I love Orson dearly and he has been a great influence on my work for many years now. I played Prince Hal on the stage with him in Dublin after he'd found me at an audition amongst hundreds of others. He always said, 'One day you and I will do the film together.'"

Orson Welles and Ginette Spanier, we both recognized the potential talent and star quality in that unknown young actor called Keith Baxter.

I remember going with Hugh Beaumont to the National Theatre production of *The Three Sisters*. I was staying with him in his beautiful house in Westminster. We were so excited by our evening that we sat up half the night talking. Never had we seen, we agreed, a greater Masha than Joan Plowright; and Laurence Olivier's production had somehow given us a new vision of the play, as if we were seeing it for the first time—we who knew it so well and had seen it so often. From there we got to discussing the Russian character. Binkie was surprised at how deeply I understood it. He had not realized that my husband comes from a Russian family. Amazing that Paul-Emile should be so French with that background, but then he was born in Paris and has never been to Russia. Anyway, I've had plenty of opportunity to study Russian psychology, especially that of the middle-class intellectuals, who haven't changed all that much since Tchekov. The vanity of their misery, of their constant exhaustion— exactly like *The Three Sisters*. They are the greatest intellectual snobs in the world, that type of Russian. Somehow they feel it is deep and intellectual to be unhappy, to be poor, to suffer; they feel it slightly degrading to feel well, to feel happy, to be successful. My parents-in-law were like that. This made them very difficult to get on with, especially for someone like me, whose instincts all tend towards optimism and physical and mental well-being. And there was an added problem: Paul-Emile was an only son, and tall and handsome and brilliant into the bargain. Beware, girls who dare approach an only son! The man-eating mother is a terrifying creature. I arrived in Paris to face married life full of idiotic illusions and found myself subjected to a pretty intensive course of torture. I had always been surrounded by so much warmth and love in my life, and suddenly I encountered hatred—for the first time. It found me quite unprepared. Three months after my arrival in Paris came the war, and I was cut off from everything I loved—from my family, from my friends, from my country. My father-in-law was killed in an accident, and we took Paul-Emile's mother to live with us as we wandered all over France hiding from the Germans. Through it all, her attitude towards me did not alter by one iota. My solitude during those war years was stark. It put steel into any inner strength I possessed. My mother-in-law died after the war, but inside of me the wounds have never completely healed.

I start thinking back . . . when was it that I saw myself in print for the first time? Surely before *It Isn't All Mink*? What was it? The little golden fish gleams for a minute on the surface and disappears. To hell with my moth-eaten memory! Then it comes back . . . I know—"Letter from Paris" in the *Sunday Times*. However did that come about? I feel my way back painfully along that tenuous Ariadne's thread which is spun from my souvenirs. . . . Got it. Ian. Ian Fleming. Dear, impossible, attractive Ian.

The first time I met Ian Fleming was years ago. Noël Coward had a house right down by the sea at St. Margaret's Bay. Paul-Emile and I went to spend the weekend there, and I remember that all three of us—Noël, Paul-Emile and I—travelled from Paris to Dover by the lovely Golden Arrow. That was comfort. And leisure. And luxury. The slow lunch on the French train; that first English drink in one's cabin on the boat with Springgay, the purser, his gold-braided cap worn at an angle (he had known me since I was was 12, which was when I started travelling backwards and forwards across the Channel).

I loved Noël's house at St. Margaret's Bay, the sea all around—almost lapping at the garden gate, the green grass right down to the shingle, the cross-Channel steamers outside our windows, the wind, the sea air.

Noël had lent the cottage next to his house to Ian Fleming.

This particular weekend came at the time of Ian's romance with Ann Rothermere (whom he married some time later), and he was acting up like mad to the mystery of the situation. He strode in from next door soon after we arrived, spectacularly good-looking in his rugged way. Gorgeous clothes. Dressed as only an Englishman knows how to dress in the country; all so seemingly casual. Offhand to the point of rudeness, he never addressed a single word to anybody but Noël. Paul-Emile and I might have been made of transparent vinyl.

In 1954 Paul-Emile and I went to spend Christmas with Noël Coward in Jamaica, and Noël took us over to lunch at 'Goldeneye', Ian Fleming's house a few miles away. This time I penetrated Ian's consciousness, and he was enchanting. Noël was always terribly rude about 'Goldeneye'. He called it 'Golden Eye, Nose and Throat', complained unceasingly about the food, and was furious because the wooden banquettes on which one sat at the dining table were too hard and too high. Ian was worried about his writing. He'd reached an *impasse*, and I remember Noël speaking to him very seriously.

"Go on writing," he said. "You write very well. Don't let your wife's intellectual friends laugh at you. They're jealous because you'll probably make more money than they ever will."

This, at the time, seemed a ridiculous statement. Ian as a writer was unknown. The James Bond mystique was far from having broken on the world.

What would any of us do without Noël's advice and wisdom at the difficult moments of our lives?

Later, in Paris, I received an unexpected telephone call from Ian Fleming in London. He told me the *Sunday Times*, of which he was Foreign Manager, was looking for someone to follow Nancy Mitford for their "Letter from Paris", and Noël Coward had suggested me. I was delighted at the idea, although I had never written for a newspaper in my life. Ian told me to write a dummy article and to post it to him in Jamaica.

I set to work on the dummy and sent it off to him.

By return came a three-page manuscript letter headed 'Goldeneye', Oracabessa, Jamaica, and starting, "I think the dummy is excellent." Then he went on to show me where I had gone wrong, to give me pertinent, detailed advice: "Keep notes during the month. They are vital. And each piece should be crammed with facts and news—new slang words, new jokes, and the *dessous* of things." And he ended by telling me to start again and send him a second dummy.

Helpful, encouraging letters followed. Ian took trouble over every detail even to the title of the articles. The last letter ended: "After this long coaching letter I shall now step out of the picture and leave you to sink or swim with the editor who, in any case, would much prefer to have direct *contact* (I bet!) with you." The *italic* is Ian's, so is the corny remark—the whole thing terribly Ian.

And shortly after, there appeared in the *Sunday Times* an article headed "Sous les Toits de Paris by Ginette". I was immeasurably proud and excited. So was my whole family. I kept the job for about a year.

Ever after, Ian Fleming and I were friends in a casual way, but friends just the same. I had a very soft spot in my heart for him. What woman hadn't? He often talked terrible nonsense, and I would tell him so, and we'd argue and laugh. He would drop in to see me at Balmain's, and we'd go across the road for a drink; and Ian would shout at me because I encouraged Annie, his wife, to buy clothes.

(*above*) At Cape Kennedy in the Space Museum. G. Spanier is fascinated and is wearing a brown jacket trimmed with white and brown mink. November 1968

Photo: *Arnold Weissberger*

(*above*) With Maurice Chevalier. (*below*) My big evening in Chester. In the Town Hall with The Bishop of Chester and Mr. and Mrs. Leonard Harris

Madame la Directrice. At Pierre Balmain's

I remember once when I was in England, Ian Fleming and Nancy Spain had been out together playing golf, and they came to fetch me at my parents' house in Golders Green. It was during my father's last illness. Both Ian and Nancy went up to his bedroom and put themselves out to entertain him.

My father, as was his way when he was having a good time, said, "Come on. Let's open a bottle of champagne!"

A bottle was brought up. My father loved 'occasions'.

The ride back to the West End with those two pirates in Ian's famous Thunderbird was a joyous one. They had a lot in common Ian and Nancy: both had *panache*. Both loved *choquer le bourgeois*. Both were difficult and brilliant and immensely kind underneath. Both were in love with journalism and the Navy (they had both been in the Navy during the war). Both were 'mad about Lord Beaverbrook and Noël Coward'. Both were second children in families where the eldest had received preferential treatment from the mother. Both were unhappy at school: Ian at Eton and Sandhurst; Nancy at Roedean, which she had loathed. She had begged her parents to take her away from that mock-Gothic monstrosity on the Sussex Downs, but they wouldn't. She used to speak about it to me for hours. Both Ian and Nancy at school had, with a kind of bravado, run away with many of the prizes "just to show them".

Both Nancy and Ian were larger than life, and I loved them for it. Gilbert Harding was too. They all three belonged to that particular breed of English personality, so dear to the heart of the great British public: unfailing humour, more than a dash of outrageousness, those are the requisite ingredients. I remember once driving in an open car down Regent Street with Nancy Spain and Gilbert Harding, and the bus conductors, the people on the buses, the taxi drivers shouting, "Hello, Nance!" "Hello, Gilbert!" A royal progress.

I met Gilbert Harding when I appeared for the very first time on a big radio programme. Gilbert was one of the

I

participants. His fame at the time was immense. I was shaking with nerves. Before we started, Harding, very sweetly, gave me some invaluable advice; and after I had done my piece he took out his gold pencil, leaned over and wrote, "*Magnifique, Madame!*" on my paper. After the show we went out to lunch, and Gilbert Harding, a great *raconteur*, talked and talked and talked.

Lately I have met another of these outsize personalities— Lord Boothby. I was booked to take part in the radio programme, "Any Questions".

Nancy Spain used to say to me: "That is one programme you'll never get on to, you who take absolutely no interest in world affairs." But there I was, standing outside Bath station waiting for a BBC car to take me to Glastonbury, from where "Any Questions" was being broadcast that evening. I had no idea that my travelling companion on this drive was to be Lord Boothby. I had never met him. Before we'd left the station yard I was laughing.

As we drove along the beautiful Somerset roads, Boothby said, "We can't be far from Wells."

"Wells Cathedral?" I asked. "I've never seen it."

"We'll go there," said Boothby. "It is the number one most beautiful cathedral in England." And to Wells we went. It was a perfect winter evening: pale, cloudless sky and a flamingo-pink sunset. We got to the cathedral as the little figures came out and struck the bell above the big clock on the hour. Then we went into the cathedral. It was dark after the twilight outside. We were alone. Suddenly unseen children's voices sang out into the silence. A moment I shall never forget.

A sexton appeared, came over and said, "My Lord, would you like to attend the service?" Boothby accepted, and we were led into the choir, which was brilliantly lit, its tapestries glowing behind the dark wooden stalls, the choir boys in their surplices and little stiff collars, the Bishop of Bath and Wells in his purple, sitting in his chair—or is it called a throne? My new friend and I were the only 'civilians'.

When we resumed our journey, Lord Boothby said, "Now you must see Glastonbury Abbey."

Night had fallen when we got there. The gates were locked. Nothing daunted, we tried to break in. The caretaker came out furious, but he finally opened the gates when he discovered that the would-be trespasser was the famous Lord Boothby. So, by the light of an electric torch, I was shown Glastonbury Abbey.

And on, at last, to Freddy Grisewood and "Any Questions". . . .

Lincoln Cathedral is one of my favourite cathedrals. I was on my way to speak at Woodhall Spa when suddenly, from the train, I saw it for the first time, up there golden in the mist. Three slender towers stretching up. Unreal and moving in the evening light.

I had asked my agent to try and get me a job in Lincolnshire because that is where Joanie Olivier comes from. Joan Plowright is one of the people I respect, quite apart from loving her as a person and admiring her as an actress. She had so often spoken to us of Scunthorpe where she was brought up, of Brigg where she was born. I wanted to have a look at the country which had given birth to her.

I got out of the train at Lincoln and drove across the flat Lincolnshire plain to Woodhall Spa. A melancholy, lonely drive as night was falling. And then the warmth and gaiety of the evening. It was the yearly 'do' of the Ladies Luncheon Club to which they invite their husbands. Everyone in evening dress. I was the cabaret.

A red-haired man came up to me. Told me he was an Australian. Had been a pilot during the war. Charming he was. Told me he'd read my book. Strange, an Australian pilot reading *It Isn't All Mink*. It meant a great deal to him, he said. Stranger still. "Do you remember," he said, "describing the first Allied air raid over Italy when you were hiding in the French Alps?" I did. Very clearly I did. "And your husband saying 'Up there are free men who can say what they think?'" Yes, I remembered. Very clearly I remembered. "I was one of those men," he said.

I was carried back twenty-four years to Notre Dame de Bellecombe, that tiny, solitary mountain village in Savoy. The cold. The wooden chalet. Ice in the jug and basin. Snow everywhere—which was good, because if there was enough snow the Germans would not dare come up the valley. Night. The silence.

Suddenly noise everywhere. Unidentifiable. Unknown. Immense noise filling the silence of the valley, echoing from the mountains. We rushed on to the wooden balcony. Nothing that we could see. Freezing cold. Clear sparkling sky. And Paul-Emile saying, "It must be the English going to bombard Italy."

And I suddenly found myself sobbing, deep down racking sobs, to think of friends within hearing distance after an eternity of isolation.

Paul-Emile took me in his arms and said, "Up there are free men who can say what they think."

And I prayed "O God please protect them. Please protect them. May they all get home safely. Please."

And now I was in Woodhall Spa, Lincolnshire, England, talking to a red-haired Australian. Twenty-four years later. In evening dress.

"The mountains looked so beautiful, gleaming white, from up there," he said. "We were the 47th Squadron. I was decorated by the King after the raid. After the war I went back to Australia, but then I came back to England and settled in Woodhall Spa, and this is where I had to come to meet one of the people who was down there in those mountains on that night."

"I prayed for you," I said.

His name is W. Astley Cooper.

I'll never get over my hatred of the Germans. My fear of their latent propensity for disciplined sadism is my only political dogma. When we drove for the first time to Scandinavia for our holidays, Paul-Emile said the shortest route was to cross Germany. I made a terrible fuss, but, at last, I gave in on condition I did not sleep on German soil, so we spent the night in the last village in Holland before the frontier. I remember the frontier barrier, and my first sight since the Occupation of that long, grey overcoat and high, peaked cap. All smiles and *Velkom* he was, that officer, who, a few short years before, with that same smile, would have sent me to the gas chamber. Instinctively, exactly as I had done during those four years when I crossed his brothers daily in the street, my head held high, I looked through him as if he were transparent. As soon as we were out of sight, I burst into tears. I couldn't stop.

My second condition to putting a foot in Germany was that we should go to Bergen Belsen. I wanted to stand and say a prayer on the spot where but for the Grace of God. . . .

Only the other day I was looking at athletics on television. A German, having won a gold medal, stood on the high place of the Podium whilst his national anthem was being played: *Deutschland Über Alles!* I was livid with rage all by myself there in my sitting-room. It reminded me of the first time the Germans came after the war to the Théatre des Nations. Every summer in Paris we have an International Theatre Festival. I did not want to go to the German show, but was persuaded this was a prejudiced, unintelligent attitude, and that I was getting rather tedious. At the start of the performance they struck up *Deutschland Über Alles.* This hymn had been banned at the end of the war but, in spite of that, the Germans elected to play it here in Paris on their first visit. Everyone stood up—except me. I shall be everlastingly grateful to Paul-Emile, who, on seeing his wife rooted to her seat, sat right down again amidst the startled and disapproving glances of the chic Parisian audience. It is quite difficult 'to go against the tide', and, after this weak attempt at breaking a lance for my principles, that heroine Ginette Spanier shook like a leaf for a good ten minutes.

Amongst my faults, proudness, which is quite different

from pride, is not one of them. I am irritable, impatient, violent and plenty of other things. Now and then I am 'pleased with myself', like when I make somebody laugh or I've been good on television, but only very occasionally am I proud of myself.

I was proud when the BBC in their "Snags" series, "The Snags of Being Famous", "The Snags of Being Beautiful", etc., chose me to do a piece on "The Snags of Being Jewish". I, Ginette Spanier, have personally never found snags to being Jewish.

I had never felt Jewish until the Germans occupied France. Being Jewish had never made the slightest difference to my life, either in England or in France. We were not brought up as Jewish. We never, as children, went to synagogue. We went to prayers at school. Nobody had ever, and I mean ever, treated me any differently from anybody else because I was Jewish. Some of my friends were Jewish. Many weren't. I just never thought about it.

When things started going badly in Germany for the Jews, I was angry but not really involved. I am ashamed of this now. I'm afraid selfishness can be added to my list of faults.

The moment the Germans occupied France, I knew I was Jewish, and that feeling has never left me since.

Once, during the Occupation, we were staying with the de Havilands, the porcelain family, in their beautiful château just outside Limoges. The Havilands did not know us: they just took us in to harbour us, to save the lives of two hunted strangers, risking their own lives in so doing. We'd been recommended to them by a clergyman. As we did not want continually to intrude upon the privacy of our hosts, Paul-Emile and I would go out and have lunch in a little bistro on the outskirts of the village. We walked quietly through that Limousin village on our way to and from lunch.

Some French villagers noticed us and thought, "Who

are those two? Why are they staying in the big house and not lunching there? They could be Jews." And they denounced us to the Gestapo on the chance of the reward. People received a few francs a Jew from the Germans; sometimes the Germans would throw in a radio set as an extra bonus if they were short of Jews.

God warned me that day. He made me panic-stricken for the only time during the war. For no reason whatsoever I insisted on our fleeing from the house. We didn't even say good-bye to the Havilands. Precisely half an hour after our departure the Gestapo came and searched the house. I may say—and I want to state it most forcibly—that in over four years, with all the people we mixed with and who knew we were endangering their lives by being with them, with all the people we met, all the people who took us in and saved us and fed us and looked after us, this was the only time we were denounced. Our gratitude to all those other hundreds is boundless.

Still, the fact remains that there had been human beings willing to send Paul-Emile and me to unbelievable torture and a hideous death because they thought we might possibly be Jews, we who were walking quietly through a village.

That makes one feel Jewish for life, because one realizes that this sort of thing has gone on for over 5,000 years and is still going on at this very moment. How can one help but have a feeling of solidarity with every other Jew in the world?

This has nothing to do with religion—absolutely nothing. I do not know very much about the Jewish religion. I believe deeply in God. Not in a Jewish God. I believe in an all-embracing deity. But I feel part of the Jewish *race*, of that there is no doubt.

Strangely enough, in this complicated, difficult business of being Jewish, Danny Kaye, without knowing it, helped to add the last dimension to the pattern.

This is how we met. I came into Balmain's after lunch one day—this was many years ago—and started things going for the showing of the Collection. Two people were sitting near my desk, instead of being in the Salon ready to look at the show: he was red-haired and tall and wore a navy raincoat, she was short, dark and had on a mink coat. I asked one of the girls why they were there. She answered that they were Americans who had asked for Monsieur Balmain. Monsieur Balmain had been told.

I said, "Are the mannequins ready? Are the lights on? Is the girl who announces at the microphone? O.K., let's go."

And the Collection started. Still those Americans sat there, looking disconsolate.

I again called one of the girls.

"Somebody must do something about those Americans," I said. "Who are they anyway?"

"*Il s'appelle* Danny Kaye," was the answer.

In those days we had never seen him in France.

I jumped up. Only a week before, in London, Paul-Emile and I had tried to get into the Palladium. The man at the Box Office had laughed at us. Everyone in London had been talking of the great, the inimitable, the unique Danny Kaye. It had made me rather cross. Such a fuss. But now, here he was, sitting there by my desk and nobody was looking after him.

I rushed over to him and I said, "I'm terribly sorry you've been kept waiting. I'll see that Monsieur Balmain comes down straight away."

Danny Kaye looked me over in his seemingly bored, casual way.

"A British broad," he said.

"How did you know?" I asked.

"You said 'straight away'. If you'd been American, you'd have said 'right away'."

Then this red-headed man asked me my name, and "what a British broad was doing in a French joint."

"I am married to a Frenchman," I said.

What did my husband do?

"He's a doctor."

An extra gleam of interest shone for a moment in those blue, blue eyes. I did not know then that Danny Kaye was passionately interested in anything to do with the medical profession.

He kept on looking at me quizzically.

And, finally, he asked, "Is your husband's name Spanier?"

"No," I answered. "Seidmann."

"That makes sense," he said. "Come on now, let's leave this joint and go and meet that doctor husband of yours."

This unimportant, amusing incident took place not very long after the end of the war during which the fact of our being Jewish had made lepers out of us. And here was this fascinating man who seemed to take an extra interest in us *because* we were Jewish. This was something to which we were not accustomed.

We hardly ever see Danny Kaye now, but as far as I am concerned he's been a help. In some strange way he tipped the scales. On the Jewish score, inside me, I am at peace; I do not only accept wholeheartedly being Jewish—I am proud of it.

10

How Robert Would Have Laughed!

I am amazed when I hear of people who have no ambition. This attitude to life is precisely the opposite of mine. I cannot remember the time when I did not, with burning intensity, want to be first in anything I undertook. (Not, I hasten to add, that I always succeeded.) I have always loved work—as long as it had a purpose: achievement was the thing.

My first real responsibility was given to me by Deedee, our beloved governess, who understood everything about me, not least this longing for a job totally on my own. We still lived in Paris at the time. I was about 8. My little sister Janine, our pride and joy, was just born. Deedee made me 'Mistress of the Carriage'. The pram was my entire responsibility. Our apartment was on the fourth floor; the pram was kept in a little hut in the courtyard. I

would proudly go down the stairs by myself every morning—the lift was forbidden me—and I cleaned, dusted and
polished the pram till it shone. I took this job with the
utmost seriousness. Now I come to think of it, I have
always taken all my jobs with the utmost seriousness. I was
already of a very sociable disposition, and as I polished I
gossiped with the neighbours. There was Monsieur Rouet,
the chemist: he had a beard, and his duties, besides mixing
potions, included the developing of photographs. On the
sill of his back window negatives would float in mysterious
dishes, the pictures gradually taking shape almost under
our eyes. On the other side was the lace shop. In her back
room by the window the *dentellière* sat at work, mending
pieces of priceless lace. In those days, we all had lace everywhere. Great lace curtains over the windows so that the light
only filtered in; lace tablecloths hanging down to the floor
when tea was brought in by Jeanne the maid, dressed in
black with spotless white cuffs and collar and apron. Lace
doylies under the *petits fours*; even to our underwear, which
was never under any circumstances trimmed with imitation
lace.

My second real job was during the First World War. We
had moved to England by then, and Didine and I, 12 and 9
respectively, did *grown-up* war work. It seems hard to
believe. It was at the Y.M.C.A. canteen in Warren Street
which was organized by friends of my father's. I suppose
they could get nobody to work the early morning shift, so,
regularly, we two sisters, feeling that the responsibility of
the whole war rested on our shoulders, would take the
first Tube from Golders Green to Warren Street and serve
tea and cocoa out of thick white cups, and pork pies and
buns to the Tommies, who made a great fuss of us. We
took in the money, we worked the till, we gave back
change. It was my first taste of the kind of work that had
an object and achieved something in a grown-up way.
Not like school. The pleasure I derived from that kind of
work then has never lost its savour for me throughout the

years. Still, now, at the mention of a new job, of new work of any sort, I prick up my ears, I become excited and I long to have a bash at it, whatever it is, running a bar or a launderette.

But, looking back on our war work of half a century ago, it seems terribly out of Spanier character: we were so carefully brought up. That adventure must have been arranged by our father. I wonder how he got Mother to agree.

We were a very gay family, but there was a claustrophobic atmosphere about some aspects of our life. What was 'done', what 'wasn't done'. Why had I said such and such a thing? Why had I done this and that? What would people think? *What would people think?* This was the dragon which haunted my mother's life. (My father, I must be fair, minded less, but Mother won.)

From the age of 3 this attitude goaded me to paroxysms of rage. It still does. (Nobody ever changes, this I believe most strongly. They may learn to hide their feelings, but inside, they never change.) I cannot understand how people can give importance to the supposed opinion of their neighbours. I really believe that I do not mind what 'people' think of me. If some disapprove and it makes a difference to their feelings towards me—out, and good riddance. Those I love and who really love me take the package deal, good and bad, the real me. Just as I do with them. How boring this constant approving and disapproving. Conceited too. Thinking they know best. Trying to change people. Missionary stuff. Impertinent really.

Then, in our family there was not only the question of outer independence but of inner independence. In my youth I could not understand why it was that I had to conform to a philosophy of life (I did not put it quite like that then) which was alien to me. Why should I like what my mother liked? I was *me*. To my mother, nothing ever existed outside of her family. Mother never took an interest in books, music, travel. She had few real friends outside the family—her family was her whole life. And it never entered her head that we might be different. She had absolutely no respect for our privacy. It never occurred to her that we might want it. Privacy, to my mother, meant privacy from the outside world, not our own individual privacy within the family. I loved the outside world.

We were expected to show her our letters. Not that she thought there might be something wicked in them. Wickedness, to mother, meant sex and she never imagined that any of her three daughters would be touched by that form of horridness. Touch wood! Mother just could not conceive that there were things, quite innocent things, we might want to keep to ourselves, that we did not want to share with the family. Everything was discussed, picked over. Unimportant, silly incidents assumed ridiculous proportions. "Why did she say that? Surely that's very strange. It would have been more normal to say this . . ." More *normal*. This constant criticism. This constant picking. It enraged me. My friends were *mine*. My letters were sacred. I felt that once the family had picked at one of my letters, had analysed one of my friends, they had been violated, the essence of them taken from me. Like in a strip cartoon when devastation has passed by and only the bones of the fish remain, the flesh having vanished.

Father was different. He joined noisily in the family discussions, he shouted a lot; but he had other interests as well. First amongst which was earning the family living. He loved the excitement of business (we really had a lot in common). He was a gambler. (I, on the other hand, am allergic to gambling.) He had very strong views on politics. He read, in a prejudiced way. He loved gardening. Music was his great love: Mozart, Kathleen Ferrier, the classics brought him joy until the day of his death at the age of 89. He was undefeatedly optimistic, and his enthusiasm knew no bounds. He was embarrassingly proud of us.

We were a very shouty family. I remember blazing rows, with both sides word perfect, driving each other to an irritation beyond control. My sister Didine does not remember any of this and thinks I make it up. But then Didine was such a darling. I was poisonous. I remember, even in the nursery, accepting with difficulty the mores of my 'milieu'. For my independence I would have fought unto death. I was untamed in those days, and I had worked out a routine: my mind was quick and my lungs were strong so, by guessing how to annoy, and screaming louder than most—my mother worried as to what the neighbours might think of the terrible noise—I managed, if not to get it all my own way, at least to make myself pretty much of a pest, which is a form of victory.

Sex was rigidly excluded from the family. The question was never referred to. We three girls were never told a thing. But the fear of this unmentionable, unmentioned Thing lurked in the corners.

Apart from this exasperating *bourgeois* side, my mother brought us up with great good sense: never was any fuss made about our health, for one. It wasn't interesting to be ill, and even now it hardly ever occurs to us to take our temperature. Also, it wasn't clever to be shy. "If you feel shy, swallow it," my mother used to say, although she herself was an intensely shy woman. I must say I agree with her. Those who pride themselves on being shy, they bore me and I don't trust them, alongside the ones who talk in whispers. Uriah Heep forms of arrogance. Two other principles impressed upon us in our youth have stuck hard: tidiness and a hatred of laziness. Both Didine and I hate untidy rooms, untidy people, untidy minds, and laziness does not enter the Spanier conception of things. This has been a great help to us in life.

To sum it all up: there was laughter, there was fun, there was noise, there were weak attempts at revolt, but the result, nonetheless, was a family hothouse, a hothouse which protected us from the *real* world. And that kind of hothouse, however much one thinks one longs for adventure, is hard to get away from mentally. I always feel that had I been brought up in a less sheltered atmosphere, had I remained untamed, I might have done great things. Maybe had we had a brother, it would have been different. I longed passionately for a brother.

I don't feel in the least sentimental about my childhood, in fact I usually rather shy away from the thought of it. Not like Paul-Emile, who likes to wallow in early souvenirs, who adored his schooldays, who loves to talk of long past incidents in his life. I give a passing salute to 37 rue Ampère, the house where I was born, every time I pass it on my way to Le Bourget Airport, and there it ends.

But once one starts to remember, so many things come crowding back. Take lamp-lighters. Yes, I remember them. In my childhood the lights of the city did not go on all together in one great blaze at the pressing of an unseen button. Each street lamp was lit individually. At dusk, the lamp-lighters would foregather by a bench in a little square a few minutes from where we lived. I seem to remember they wore butcher-blue smocks and, I suppose, caps of some kind: in those days nobody went out bare-headed. And they carried long poles. They were friendly characters, not like the postmen who lounged outside the Post Office shouting remarks and who frightened me terribly.

After a little chat among themselves, the lamp-lighters separated and each went on his allotted way. At every lamp-post the lamp-lighter stopped. With his long pole, he would flick a little knob high up in the lamp, there would be a splutter, and the light came on. And on to the next lamp-post went the lamp-lighter.

Another thing I remember very clearly was that summer in Pourville near Dieppe when I was 7. Summer holidays in those days were endless. Whole lives in their own right. We lived in a big rambling villa called 'Mi-Côte', meaning half-way up the hill. It was filled with foreign relatives from all over Europe. A hot, breathless summer. We went shrimping and bathing in long striped bathing dresses and white cotton hats. We had to splash water on our foreheads and on our chests as we entered the sea for protection against sunstroke; and, of course, we were forbidden to bathe for at least two hours after lunch for fear of seizures during digestion. My mother wore a black alpaca bathing dress with a full skirt, and black stockings. On her head like a *madras* she tied a pale blue triangle of waterproof satin. She looked beautiful. I didn't enjoy bathing. I was frightened. One day on the beach there was an invasion of jelly-fish.

Our lovely bachelor uncle was over from America, and the ladies flirted with him. We hated them. We loved him. With the exception of my uncle and perhaps my father, we did not think much of the grown-ups, with their jokes which we did not understand. We were happiest just the three of us, Deedee, my little sister Didine and me—a tight little knot of interwoven loyalty against the world. There were as yet only two Spanier sisters in those days. Janine, the baby, was to come later. She is the one who left us the first. She died of polio in India during the war. Didine is three years younger than me. An English cousin with us that summer called her 'a little brown bundle'. She was small and sweet and good and had two teeth too many so that her smile with all those tiny white teeth was the smile of a little brown mouse.

We went for walks when the sun wasn't too hot, or sat under the trees in the shade. I remember the smell of hot grass, and the noise of bees, and looking at insects scuttling in the grass. We had a private hideaway, a hut we called 'Petite Mi-Côte', which looked out on an endless golden cornfield with red poppies. I was reminded of it when I saw that wonderful film *Oh What a Lovely War*. I remember our disgust if one of the grown-ups dared to trespass on our private property, especially those terrible flirty ladies.

The grown-ups took up golf—a very *chic*, English thing to do—and now and then, we children, brushed and polished, were taken up to the clubhouse for tea. The golf course was high up on the cliffs overlooking the sea, where

England was on the other side. I've never stopped loving green grass high up over the sea.

Sometimes a little English boy called Archie came to the clubhouse, and I fell in love with him. He must have been all of 9 years old, fair hair, socks to his knees, grey flannel little boy's suit—or have I dressed him like that in my memory? Once, very shyly, I said "Good afternoon" to him with my French accent. That was the beginning and end of our intimacy. I longed to have him as a friend, an English friend. Deedee used to talk to him in English. One day Archie fell and his knee was all bloody, but he did not shed a tear. We could see the effort he was making not to cry.

And Deedee said to us, "You see, in England one never cries when one is hurt. If one does, one is a coward." And she explained to us that a coward was a shameful and dreadful thing. Because of Archie, my sister Didine has never been able to cry, even in a cinema.

Another thing Deedee tried to cure me of was jealousy. She said to me with the hint of an Irish brogue, "You have a terrible jealous nature. This is very ugly. If there is nothing you can do about it, at least keep it inside yourself and don't let anybody know."

Deedee was right, I was a very jealous little girl. Never envious—but jealous.

Jealousy is the ugliest, the most destructive, the most horrible, the most painful emotion in the world. It can never be really cured, however much one tries. Like a disgusting weed it proliferates unseen and pops up again when least expected. Thank Heaven for old age. Surely old age must eliminate the occasions on which jealousy breeds.

So, early on, although I had a violent nature, I tried to swallow and hide deep down inside me the shaming things about myself. This, when I grew older, resulted in a good old mess, as near as needs be to a nervous breakdown. The first thing I did when I started earning my living was to go to a psychoanalyst for help. Psychoanalysis cleared out a

K

lot of the difficult problems inside me and made it possible for me to exist with myself (although never, at any time, had anyone realized I had found it difficult). This was many years ago when psychoanalysis was an unending adventure and my psychoanalysis was just about as much agony as anything could be. It went on for years and years. One of the reasons it went on for so long was that my first analyst, a famous doctor, one day when I was lying on the couch trying to winkle out of my innermost me something very painful, fell asleep. I heard a snore behind my head. That sent me hurtling back to the beginning just like a game of snakes and ladders.

However, in spite of the long-drawn-out pain of my analysis, I am grateful to Mr. Freud. Psychoanalysis is not only a cure, it is also a great mental and intellectual exercise. It taught me to think clearly and without camouflage, to judge people objectively and, most important of all, never again was I able to fool myself on the subject of me.

But the psychoanalysis did not cure me of one dreadful fear: water. I never trusted water. Early in my youth I suffered one of the most humiliating experiences of my whole life. This was soon after we had moved to England from France. I was about 12, and with my two sisters, we were sent to Frognal School in Hampstead.

On Wednesday mornings we went to the Hampstead Baths in Finchley Road and there were taught to swim. In that damp, dank, smelly place, first with a string around our middle, and then without, it was 'push-two-three' until we could vaguely keep afloat. After this dismal weekly ritual, up the arid heights of Netherhall Gardens and Fitzjohns Avenue, we would climb back to school in a crocodile. I loathed Wednesday mornings. But worse was still to come. The girls of the lower third got to the jumping stage. One after the other as the whistle went, they ran along the springboard and—*in*, noses pinched, legs wildly flying, like frogs. Until it came to Jenny Spanier. The

whistle blew. I ran. I got to the end of the springboard.
And stopped—like a mule. Back I went, death in my heart.
Again I ran. Again I couldn't. I stopped dead. By the third
time the whole lower school was standing around shouting,
"Jump Frenchie." But it was impossible.

I was a coward.

The terrible shame of that morning stayed with me and
burnt into my soul. Yet in all the years that followed I
never had the guts to jump or dive into the water and
break the curse. My sister Didine became a champion
diver, but I would creep down the steps if it was a swimming pool or boat, or walk gingerly in bit by bit if it was a
beach. Then I'd swim around 'push-two-three' like a timid
mouse.

Until a few years ago when I was quite old I went to
Greece for my summer holiday. To the Island of Hydra. I
stayed in a white house high up in that village of steps, a
guest of Gordon Merrick the author and Charles Hulse.
The sun was hot and golden, the sea was warm and blue,
and bathing was a joy. But I still crept down into the sea,
toe first, whilst everyone else dived triumphantly from
caïque or rocks. At last I could bear it no longer. Beautiful
Theodoros, the swaggering, brown-eyed boatman, threw a
piece of bread into the water from the boat, and made
signs to me which meant, "Get it." (I don't speak Greek.)
There was a terrible plop and, after half a century of fear,
Jenny Spanier had gone into the sea head first!

That was only the beginning. The next year I went to
Greece again. Again the white house with the four white
terraces high up on the Island of Hydra, and the golden sun
and the blue sky and blue sea and my two handsome hosts.
And a 36-foot sloop had replaced the *caïque*. I decided to
have done for ever with fear and shame and silly fuss. By
the end of the holiday I had conquered. In, out, from the
lowest bit of the deck, from the highest bit of the deck,
before breakfast, after midnight, I dived into the warm
Greek sea, and in so doing, I discovered the joy and elation

of the physical life. And at an age when on the stage I would be portrayed sitting in a bath chair with an ear trumpet.

On my way home from Greece I passed through London, and as I drove along Finchley Road I saw that workmen were at work demolishing the Hampstead Baths. Revenge was mine! I had won.

The Hampstead Baths! Frognal School! I wasn't unhappy at school but I was totally uninspired. There was no excitement in our studies. Rivalry was not encouraged. I longed to be at a school where there was competition. As a matter of principle there were no first and seconds—so I had no real interest in the proceedings. I had no incentive to push me on. And the stupidity of the questions; the soul-killing effort of trying to work out the square root of a number on a motor car plate or how quickly a bath would fill up from two different taps. Who cared? Who did it help?

Then one day, in the basement of Fortnum and Mason's, on the first day of my first job, I was called upon to expend the same kind of energy, but in selling trays on which a lot of pink gentlemen chased after a fox and, at the end of the week, I received a lovely cheque for my pains. That made sense. It was the Y.M.C.A. all over again.

Work is work—very enjoyable, and leisure to me is lying in the sun. Flat in the sun. This *idée fixe* has caused much discussion with my husband when it came to holidays. His idea of a rest is to get into a car and drive day in, day out, all over Norway, looking at the scenery, which I admit is quite extraordinarily beautiful. This is not my idea of fun. Cars, especially closed cars, are to me strictly for getting from one place to another quickly. And I can't just 'look at' scenery.

I went to Scandinavia with Paul-Emile for seven years running; then realizing that, as one gets older, holidays are precious gifts not to be squandered, we decided to go our separate ways on vacation. I said good-bye to the fjords. Not for me any more: "Look at that waterfall! Isn't it beautiful? That valley. That mountain." I am not impervious to scenery. But it has to sink into me surreptitiously, to become part of me, as a background to my life. Take Notre Dame de Bellecombe in Savoy. The country round that mountain village moves me deeply. The fields and the mountains and the mud and the air became part of me when we hid there during the war. The peasants became our friends. But, beautiful though it is, had I just come across that corner of the Alps in the course of a journey it would have made no dent in my emotions. There is a sooty wall in Camden Town which turns my heart over each time I pass it because of the thoughts it brings. I'd rather have that sooty wall than an anonymous glacier with the sun setting on it.

I actively dislike the burnt brown earth and dark cypresses of Italy; I've never been happy in Italy. The whitewashed houses of Spain give me the willies: I can't see beauty where there is so much poverty. As for the hills of Provence, up which creep little flat-roofed houses crowned with ruined citadels—for my money, you can have them. Yet, take all of these together, as seen from my white terrace on the Island of Hydra, and they spell peace and beauty to me. Because I stay there weeks on end and I am happy there.

Gordon Merrick and Charlie Hulse have not only taught me to love the burnt hills of Greece, but they have brought me a joy hitherto unknown to me—sailing.

I had always hankered for boats—but, except for the odd steamer, these had rarely come my way. On my second holiday in Greece, my hosts had exchanged their apartment in Paris for *The Strumpet Wind IV* named after one of Gordon's novels. Half an hour after arriving at Athens Airport, more of an exhausted mess than usual after a year's work, I was sitting in a pair of shorts on the deck of a real yacht. A revelation.

Sailing—when the sails are rigged and the wind suddenly fills them. In this world of hideous noise, you relearn the meaning of silence. When it is calm you lie flat in the sun, the breeze all around. Complete indolence. And, suddenly, at the drop of a tiny nautical beret, all hell is let loose, and it's against God's sea and God's wind that you pit your brains and your strength and your courage. Pure exhilaration. Muscles were put to work that I did not know I possessed. It was exciting at my age to discover that I had a body, a body to which one gave orders, quite tough orders, which were carried out without too much difficulty. A body which became brown and lean from losing that beastly urban fat. A body which welcomed with gratitude the unaccustomed contact with the air and the sun and the sea.

I am often clumsy on land because I am usually thinking of other things, and I don't bother to look where I am going. In the restricted space of the boat, I learnt to be agile and careful. To keep my balance and not to make a fool of myself.

I, who all my life have suffered cruelly from insomnia—after a day at sea, I slept like a child. I, who loathe getting up in the morning—I bathed before breakfast. I, who am a fool in the kitchen—I became the perfect galley slave.

When my two friends saw how much I loved it all, they encouraged me. "How dare you heave yourself up the boat-steps with your knee? Don't be so lazy. An extra heave and your *feet* on the third rung." When I achieved it, I almost sang for joy.

From our boat deck I saw a side of Greece I would never have imagined had I travelled any other way. We explored the coast of the Peloponnese. That's how we came upon Yraka. We sailed down a crack in that arid coast and, suddenly, round a bend, a few white houses with, high up above, the remains of an Acropolis. On the quay three shops.

Tied up to the quay, from our front-row stalls, we participated in the life of that Greek village. They get their ice from Sparta. From Sparta. Enough to make one dream.

One day in Yraka there was a fight between two drunks —epic stuff. It lasted all afternoon in the glaring sunshine, with the village divided in two trying to keep the combatants apart.

There was a balcony over the poor little café opposite our moorings. Every evening after the sun had gone down an invalid was brought out from inside the house and installed on a bed set up on the balcony. We called her Jocasta, she was so regal, lying there wrapped in her black veils. Her family and neighbours would come and sit with her. They ate their frugal evening meal on the balcony by the light of an oil lamp. One night three Orthodox priests with their long hair, their high black hats and long black robes came to visit the invalid. Their shadows, immense, were projected on the wall of the house in the dark by the light of the oil lamp. Afterwards the priests were taken downstairs and offered a meal on the quay, with Jocasta shouting instructions from her balcony. She slept out on the balcony and was brought back into the house in the early morning when the sun rose, to spend the day behind the closed shutters away from the heat. One evening at a sign from Jocasta I climbed up to the balcony and paid obeisance to her who clearly ruled the village. We conversed in sign language. She made me understand that for the last two years she had been suffering from a heart condition, and, with my hands clasped, I conveyed to her my sympathy and my respect.

Before we left, one woman in the village gave me two fresh eggs. Another gave me an apricot. Another a glass of ouzo. And one—a glass of water.

So many unexpected pleasures have come to me as I grow older. Greece has been one of them, and there's also been Ireland. One day an outstanding couple came into Balmain's. He was big, with a Scots accent, authority and power rampant; she was beautiful: blue eyes, blonde, tall, elegant. Both had a sense of humour and evident *joie de vivre.* Jim and Meg Mullion. He owns ships. They live in Ireland. We got on instantly.

Once, I was in London staying at the Savoy and Nancy Spain came to take me out to dinner.

"Before we go out, we must just go upstairs for a minute to have drinks with some people I like very much," I said.

Nancy was irritated. "You're always having to go and have drinks here, there and everywhere!"

"I thought you'd enjoy them," I said. "They live in Ireland and they own a wonder horse."

"What's the name of the horse?" Nancy asked, trying not to sound interested.

"I don't remember. Sort of Latin-sounding. I think it begins with an R and ends with an A."

"Ragusa," Nancy shouted. "Hurry up. Now you're talking. Let's go."

In one of those lovely river suites, I might have been a fly on the wall. "That filly, by . . . out of. . . ." "A great mare. . . ." "Won the Derby in. . . ." I sat there delighted. Such excited, exciting talk. I hadn't realized Nancy was so knowledgeable about horses, although I did know that she had ridden all her life and that she had once staked her last penny and won a small fortune on a horse called The Bug.

Horsey talk, which I call 'out-of-into' had never before come my way. It seems somehow romantic to me. All those lovely names! Now, I even understand some of it.

From that drink on, Nancy backed Ragusa every time he ran, and she carpeted the whole of her new house on the proceeds. I opened an account with a London book-maker, backing every horse from the Mullion stable running in England. By far the most exciting moment of the week at Balmain's is the Tuesday afternoon post when with trembling hand I open my letter from Messrs. Upex of Ideal House. Over the years I haven't done so badly, although since Ragusa went to stud no other great champion has as yet appeared. But there are one or two of his children we have great hopes for. And now there is a filly named Jenny after me in those stables. Dear Jenny . . . I identify with her. I am proud of her notices: "Amazing incident" . . . "unique in racing annals". . . . Here is an extract from a newspaper cutting to tell the tale of her first race:

Amazing Incident

The Wilbraham Maiden Stakes will probably remain unique in racing annals for many a year to come, for the winner, Jenny, was the central figure in a remarkable incident. She shed the shoe from her off forefoot at some stage in the race and in some inexplicable fashion the shoe got caught in her tail, and stayed there. It was still there when she returned to the unsaddling enclosure, where it was unravelled by her astounded trainer Sam Armstrong.

After Amande had flattered in The Dip, Jenny, obviously not in the least incommoded by her peculiar circumstances finished with a great burst of speed to beat Cupid's Bow.

Also now there is a horse called Paul-Emile after my husband. We dream of his winning the Derby.

The Mullions not only introduced me to the excitement of horses, but they introduced me to Ireland. I had been in love with a mythical Ireland ever since our Irish Deedee had come into the family on my sixth birthday, but, in all those years, I had never been there except for unexpected landings at Shannon Airport. Now suddenly—because the Mullion family has sort of adopted me—I find myself feeling at home in County Kildare. The soft, soft rain, the green, green grass, the tall trees, the white railings, the mares and their foals outside my window, the, "Let's open a bottle of champagne, we must celebrate!" "Let's open a bottle of champagne, we need cheering up after losing that race!" The exaggerated charm of everyone one talks to. In Ireland nobody says, "Oh Ginette, she exaggerates so terribly!" In Ireland I've met my equals, my brothers.

I learn about horses and breeding, and starting gates, and handicaps, and five furlongs, and the poor teazer, and the great stallions. I try to take it all in, my brain working like anything. It's completely new to me. I'm getting quite good at it. I have even learnt to wear almost the right clothes for walking through the mud to go and see the horses, for the jumping during Horse Show week, for the races at Phoenix Park and the Curragh.

And then every year there is Paddy Prendergast's birthday, always celebrated after the Phoenix Stakes. Paddy, the great trainer, the most Irish of all; volatile, temperamental, sweet, moody, and, when the drink flows, so sentimental and Irish that you can't quite believe it's true. In the middle of it all, Ginette Spanier, whose family never saw a horse in their lives, dancing with trainers and jockeys and breeders and owners.

My pleasure in people and really getting to know them does not diminish, I am thankful to say, as I grow older. Not, of course, that I really *feel* any older. The years creep past, and yet I still refer to Didine as 'my little sister', which makes her furious. And now and then I talk to Noël Coward about 'the Spanier Girls', which makes *him* furious.

He says, "Why not Baby, you're not 70 yet."

But there it is, 'little sister' or no, the 'Spanier Girls' or no, there are only the two of us left from that noisy, shouty Spanier family: Didine and I, Adrienne and Jenny. And however much we may have fought in the old days, we've become very, very close, the two of us. We're opposites in character, although we look very much alike. But Didine is one of the people I can laugh with, I can talk with, one of the people with whom I am never, never bored. She is, in a sense, my sanity.

Something happened not long ago to bring the whole question of my growing old sharply into focus. I'd always suffered remorse at never giving my blood for transfusion. I'm strong and healthy, and I felt my good red blood could be of use to some less fortunate creature. But, in spite of my good intentions, I never got around to it. So, when I saw on the notice board at work an announcement of a Blood Giving Day at Balmain's, I immediately put my name down.

On that morning, with just a cup of black coffee inside me, I went up to what is usually *Le Studio* and found it transformed into a hospital: doctors and nurses in white coats, bottles, blood, phials, rubber tubing, and blood donors lying prone on pallet beds, with bandages round their arms—just like a scene from Cecil Woodham-Smith's *Florence Nightingale*. Very unexpected at Pierre Balmain's in a room usually given over to silks, satins, velvets and furs. In the room next door, where the model girls are usually fitted during the creating of the Collection, the brave blood donors were being restored with a breakfast of coffee, *croissants*, fresh rolls, butter and redcurrant jam. They all looked very impressed when *Madame la Directrice* walked in to give her precious blood.

One of the nurses started rubbing my arm with an antiseptic and sticking a needle in whilst a secretary asked me some questions.

When I got to the date of my birth she jumped up as if she'd been stung by a wasp and screamed, "You're much too old. You can't give blood at your age!"

So shocked was the nurse operating on my arm that she started in horror, and my unwanted blood spurted out in a great, beautiful red gush, soaking everything in sight. Such a waste.

This was the first time I had been told I was too old for something. It didn't upset me. It surprised me. And it made me think. As I said, I don't really feel old. I feel less young. I don't mind getting old, and I don't look all that different thanks to the help of Loving Care No. 77 on my hair.

Aches and pains and always looking for one's glasses are a bore. A terrible bore. That's certain. But what's the use of making a fuss? It doesn't help. Quite the contrary. And there are great compensations: I don't have to do a lot of things '*pour l'honneur*', like one did when one was young. If I walk into a famous restaurant with a girl-friend instead of with a man, I don't feel disgraced. When my sister Didine and I want to celebrate—it's a tradition—we go, just the two of us, to the Savoy Grill, and the *Maître d'Hôtel* gives us one of his best tables, and it's lovely, with no strings. In the old days we'd never have dared. If I want to stay at home and go to bed, I stay at home and go to bed: I'm not ashamed of not having a 'date'. I don't have to prove anything to myself or to anybody else.

I don't suffer pangs of anguish as I used to do about things like fearing I had not been a success or having said the wrong thing. Except for the necessary evils encountered in my work, I do a minimum of things I don't want to do.

So far it hasn't been like I thought at three score years. In Montherlant's play *La Reine Morte*, the King, a dodder-ing old man, grey hair, grey beard, exclaims just before dying, "*J'ai soixante ans*". (I am sixty years old.) That gives a 'girl' a shock.

No, I don't really feel old, and that's the truth. Now and then, even, I have to keep a sharp eye open not to be silly. For instance, when I am in London, although I have not lived there for almost thirty years, I fall back uncon-sciously into gestures I used to make when I was young: I hop on and off the bus as it is going. I'd better take care. I sit in the Tube thinking my thoughts, reading the old advertisements, slipping back to knowing without work-ing it out how long to the second is the interval between Belsize Park and Chalk Fram, between Golders Green and Hampstead. Into the crowded carriage comes an old lady: I have to stop myself from jumping up to give her my seat. She is probably young enough to be my daughter. I'd better be careful.

There are a whole lot of things *not* to do when you're not as young as you used to be. I look around at my contem-poraries and everywhere I see danger signals of how *not* to behave. I note that one of the tendencies common to many of my age group is to reproach. Reproaches (and cooked apples) are two of the things I really detest. "You haven't rung me lately." "Now that you're so grand, you obviously have no time for me." "You were different thirty-five years ago." Obviously I was different thirty-five years ago. Sad, if I wasn't. Time moves on, and people evolve along different lines. This is a fact, and must be accepted. "You're so grand." That boring old refrain. "Yes, I'm so bloody grand working my guts out these last thirty-five years, you'd be surprised. And, believe me, as a result, my free time is my own. To dispose of as I see fit. And no fake sentimental blackmail will get me to sacrifice one iota of it." That's *my* way of growing old. Has it never occurred to these people that the reason I don't ring them is perhaps because they bore the daylights out of me? That a flow of remonstrances as we meet does nothing to endear them to me? And that, now that I am older, I would rather be quietly at home alone than with someone who irritates me? Thirty-five years ago perhaps we had more in common. I don't remember. Maybe in those days I liked being surrounded with acquaintances? Now I like friends. If someone does not ring *me* up, I may be disappointed, but I don't *blame* them. I think, "They're bored with me. Pity." We must beware not to take ourselves too seriously as we grow old.

There's another danger signal as the years pass: the moaners and groaners about health. They pin you against the wall like a captive butterfly—some butterfly! and they start. Here go the the descriptions of their symptoms in minute detail. Never forget, all-you-who-are-not-young-any-more, that your ills interest no one. Your doctor, at least, you can pay *him* to listen. But to others, in answer to, "How do you feel?" "Fine," is the utmost you can say on the subject, whatever and however you are feeling.

In the final analysis it's not the number of years that counts, it is holding oneself straight. Very important. And not letting oneself go—especially fat. A sprightly walk helps. Not dragging one's feet if one can possibly help it. Hopping up to fetch things, and bending down to pick them up, instead of sitting there, or leaning over arm outstretched. Most important of all, is zest for life. This, thank Heaven, I have retained exaggeratedly. May it last until the end.

"How Robert would have laughed!" is a line in the play *Richard of Bordeaux* in which John Gielgud made one of his first big successes. Richard II, in prison, is sitting in his cell expecting to be murdered and thinking of the friend he loved, Robert de Vere, Earl of Oxford, exiled ten years before. I can see John Gielgud sitting there sadly, musing on the irony of the situation. He smiled, murmured, "How Robert would have laughed!" And the curtain fell. This sentence has remained with my sister and me ever since we saw the play in 1933. We've said it about so many people. Those are the people one really misses, those with whom one could laugh.

I think I can truthfully say that I am not afraid of death. The act of dying—yes, but I believe that a new, very live adventure is waiting for us round that difficult corner.

And, when I've gone, I hope that now and then there'll be a few people who will say, "How Ginette would have laughed!"